Irish Museums and Heritage Centres

HUGH ORAM

APPLETREE GUIDE

For Bernadette

First published by
The Appletree Press
19-21 Alfred Street
Belfast BT2 8DL

A catalogue record for this book is available from the British Library

ISBN 0-86281-548-7

9 8 7 6 5 4 3 2 1

INTRODUCTION

The array of museums and heritage centres that display and explain the Irish past has proliferated beyond belief during the past decade, so much so that many general-interest centres have now been complemented by an extraordinary variety of new and specialised collections. The traditional town or county museum was once the apogee of a neglected sector; now these museums make imaginative use of the most modern display and presentation techniques, the museums in Monaghan and Dundalk being fine examples of the new genre.

When the first phase of the new National Museum site opens in Dublin later in 1996, it will provide an outstanding example of new techniques being used to display venerable old collections. The Hunt Collection in Limerick is soon to have a fitting new building, the refurbished old Custom House in the city, for its collection, one of the most important in Ireland.

Many new centres, among them the Ceide Fields, the Somme Centre, the Blasket Centre, the Corlea trackway centre, Dublinia and the Waterways centre in Dublin, are all fine examples of new presentations using futuristic methods. The Boyne Valley, too, is to acquire a new centre fit for the 21st century.

At the other end of the scale, among small museums run by individuals and families there has also been much growth and expansion. Increasingly, the industrial and commercial life of the country is being preserved, with a fine emphasis on displaying the artefacts of ancient industries such as with whiskey distilling, milling and linen. Railways also feature prominently, most noteworthy being the opening of the fine new railway collection in the Ulster Folk and Transport Museum at Cultra, County Down.

This growth in museums and heritage centres is spread right throughout Ireland, North and South, a great complement to the long-established set pieces like Bunratty and the Ulster Museum. We cannot move forward and develop without a proper appreciation of the past and now, fortunately, the past is well presented in all its aspects.

***Note:** The opening hours listed under each entry are believed to be correct at the time of going to press. However, as these are liable to change, readers are advised to confirm times with the museum or centre before a visit.*

AN DÚN TRANSPORT AND HERITAGE MUSEUM

Doon, County Offaly

This museum gives a unique insight into the various methods of transport used in Ireland this century. The older methods of transport are represented by pony and trap and side-car exhibits, together with Penny Farthing bicycles and pre-World War I bicycles fitted with carbide lamps. Among the motor vehicles on display are lorries, dating from the 1920s, and a selection of farm tractors. Cars vary from the Bullnose Morris Cowley, built in the 1920s, to the more modern, but equally classic Morris Minor. Shop, café.

12 km (7 miles) SE of Athlone on the N62 to Ferbane. Admission charge. Open 10.30am-6pm Mon-Sat, 1pm-6pm Sun, Easter-Oct. Tel. (0902) 30106.

ADARE, COUNTY LIMERICK

Often regarded as Ireland's most picturesque village, Adare's **Main Street** is lined with thatched cottages. The village, which is set on the banks of the River Maigue, has changed little since the late 19th c., while several buildings are of considerable antiquity. **Desmond Castle** dates back to the 14th c., while parts of the Church of the Most Holy Trinity (Catholic) date back to the 13th c. and parts of the parish Church of Ireland church were built in the 14th c. Adare's new heritage centre uses artefacts, models and an audio-visual presentation to portray the history of Adare from its foundation in 1233. It also has craft shops and a restaurant.

16 km (10 miles) SW of Limerick.

Heritage Centre: *Admission charge. Open 9am-6pm daily, all year. Tel. (061) 396666.*

ARAN ISLANDS INTERPRETATIVE CENTRE

Inishmore, County Galway

The unique history, spirit and landscapes of the Aran Islands are well documented in this centre, standing in Kilronan, the "capital" of the islands, on Inishmore, the principal of the three islands. The centre details the geology, history and present lifestyle of the islands.

Visitors can see how the legendary currachs, those open-topped, often tar-coated, boats that skim over the waves, are made. Also on display are details of the fish species off the islands and how the islanders have long used seaweed to create patches of soil, that could be cultivated for crops, in between the dry stone walls that criss-cross the islands and divide its tiny fields. The islands' other craft traditions, including weaving of the famous Aran sweaters, are also documented. Craft shop and coffee shop. *See also Inis Oírr.*
Centre of Kilronan village, near harbour. Admission charge. Open 10am-7pm daily, Apr-Oct. Tel. (099) 61355.

ARDAGH, COUNTY LONGFORD
This entire village is an important site and its history, dating back to the church founded here in the 5th c. by St Patrick, is well recalled in the **Ardagh Heritage Centre.** The latter is one of Ireland's most attractive such centres and details in audio-visual form the ecclesiastical origins of Ardagh, moving on to the plantation of County Longford in the early 17th c. The centre, with its pine floors and white painted walls, even has a model *seanachie* (traditional storyteller) sitting in front of a turf fire and many details of local life, including the old roll books from the school that once occupied this building. Bar/restaurant.

The Fetherstone family, who rebuilt the village to a Swiss design in the 1860s (it's still one of Ireland's neatest villages), are well recalled and **Ardagh House,** where the Fetherstones lived until 1927, played host over the years to such literary figures as Oliver Goldsmith, Sir Walter Scott and Maria Edgeworth. It's 19th c. courtyard outbuildings have been turned into a museum of rural life, with stables and herb garden.
10 km (6 miles) SE of Longford.
Heritage Centre: *Admission charge. Open 9am-6pm Mon-Fri, 9am-9pm Sun, all year. Tel. (043) 75277. St Brigid's training centre museum, 0.8 km (0.5 mile) W of heritage centre. Same opening hours.*

ARDARA HERITAGE CENTRE

Ardara, County Donegal

This small West Donegal town once had a great weaving tradition, with over one hundred weavers turning out the tweeds for which Donegal is justly renowned. These skills were practised in the area for about 200 years until about 1970. Now the town's former courthouse has been turned into a heritage centre that neatly weaves the story of this craft, complete with a hand weaver working a loom. Visitors can follow the story of Donegal tweed from the shearing of the sheep to the completion of the woven cloth with the help of documentation, old photographs and models.

40 km (25 miles) NW of Donegal Town. Admission charge. Open 10am-6pm daily, all year. Tel. (075) 41262/41704.

THE ARGORY

County Armagh

This neo-classical mansion, built in the mid-1820s, is sited not far from Ardress House and is preserved by the National Trust. The dining room table is set for tea, just as it was in its Victorian heyday, while the study has the accumulation of improvements made by several successive generations, including books, Victorian light fittings and family portraits.

11 km (7 miles) W of Portadown. Admission charge. Open 2pm-6pm Sat, Sun, bank holidays, Apr-June, Sept, 2pm-6pm daily, except Tues, July, Aug. Tel. (01868) 784753.

ARKLOW MARITIME MUSEUM

Arklow, County Wicklow

This "unvarnished" collection uses no modern display techniques whatsoever, which helps enhance its authenticity. Arklow has a very fine fishing and maritime tradition. Early this century it had eighty schooners, brigs and brigantines, a tradition continued in the present day by Arklow Shipping, which has the largest Irish-flagged fleet. There's a model of Sir Francis Chichester's *Gypsy Moth III*, built in the Arklow yard of John Tyrrell & Sons. The museum also recalls the

great hardships of World War II (the "Emergency" in Ireland). A mine from this period stands at the entrance to the museum, Arklow was the first place in Ireland to have a lifeboat station, in 1826, and that proud tradition is also recalled. This delightful miscellany of material includes everything from old navigational instruments to a uniform worn by a merchant navy officer and a shoe worn by a woman passenger on the ill-fated *Lusitania*.
St Mary's Road, just before railway station. Admission charge. Open 10am-1pm, 2pm-5pm Mon-Sat, May-Sept (closed Sat, Oct-Apr) or by arr. Tel. (0402) 32484/32868.

ARMAGH
Armagh city, the ecclesiastical capital of Ireland, handsome with its green-swarded mall, is one of the most stimulating and interesting places to visit anywhere in Ireland because of the sheer diversity of its architectural and historical legacy. St Patrick's, the **Church of Ireland cathedral,** is essentially an early 19th c. restoration, but is arguably the most outstanding building in Armagh. The **Catholic cathedral,** also St Patrick's, was built between 1840 and 1904. The **library**, founded by the Anglican Archbishop Robinson in the 18th c., has manuscripts by Jonathan Swift, including that of *Gulliver's Travels,* many other rare books and registers of medieval archbishops. Near the Archbishop's Palace, the Palace Stables have been converted into a heritage centre, where 18th-c. scenes are brought to life. It also has a shop and café. **St Patrick's Trian** illustrates the Armagh story from earliest times in audio-visual form. Swift's many connections with the city are highlighted and the *Land of Lilliput,* a fantasy experience for children, is based on *Gulliver's Travels.*

Another most impressive development is the **Navan Centre,** a prehistoric site which features in the Ulster Cycle of epic myths. This series of earthworks and settlement sites was the earliest capital of Ulster and the mythology of those far-off times, Ireland in Celtic and pre-Christian times, is told superbly using audio-visual and interactive techniques, narration and display devices. The **Armagh County Museum,** in a converted schoolhouse, is highly rated among the small museums of Ireland, with a fine collection of archaeological, natural history, textile and railway items, besides examples of the work of such modern artists as AE (George Russell). Also in the Mall is the **Royal Irish Fusiliers Museum,** with a fine collection of medals and uniforms.

60 km (37 miles) SW of Belfast, 137 km (85 miles) NW of Dublin.

Robinson library: *Admission free. Open 10am-1pm, 2pm-4pm Mon-Fri, all year. Tel. (01861) 523142.*

Palace Stables: *Admission charge. Open 10am-7pm Mon-Sat, 1pm-7pm Sun, Apr-Sept, 10am-5pm Mon-Sat, 2pm-5pm Sun, Oct-Mar. Tel. (01861) 529629.*

St Patrick's Trian: *Admission charge. Open 10am-7pm Mon-Sat, 1pm-7pm Sun, Apr-Sept, 10am-5pm Mon-Sat, 2pm-5pm Sun, Oct-Mar. Tel. (01861) 527808.*

Navan Centre: *Killylea Road, 3 km (2 miles) W of Armagh, off A28. Admission charge. Open 10am-7pm daily, Apr-Aug, 10am-5pm daily, Sept-Mar, 11am-5pm Suns. Tel. (01861) 525550.*

County Museum: *Admission free. Open 10am-1pm, 2pm-5pm Mon-Sat, all year. Tel. (01861) 523070.*

Royal Irish Fusiliers Museum: *Admission free. Open 10am-12.30pm, 2pm-4pm Mon-Fri, all year. Tel. (01861) 522911.*

ATHLONE CASTLE

Athlone, County Westmeath

Athlone is at the very centre of Ireland and at the heart of much Irish history, particularly with the sieges of 1690 and 1691. The town's strategically important location is reflected in the castle, built on the banks of the River Shannon; work on the present castle began in the early 13th c. For almost 300 years, until 1970, the castle was an extension of the town's military barracks. Today, it contains an exhibition centre and a museum. The exhibition centre details the history of Athlone and the castle, while an audio-visual presentation recreates the great sieges. Athlone's military history is highlighted, as is the role of the modern day Irish Army in United Nations peacekeeping. The flora and fauna of the Shannon are also detailed, while Athlone's most famous son, John Count McCormack, forms a main highlight of the centre. McCormack, who became a world-renowned tenor, was born in a house (sign-posted) just across the bridge, in 1884 and died in Dublin in 1945. Among the items on show is his own gramophone, while his artistry is recalled splendidly in an audio-visual presentation. The folk museum in the castle has local craft artefacts, old household and dairy equipment and a reconstructed hearth. Tea room. *125 km (78 miles) W of Dublin. Admission charge. Open 10am-5.30pm daily, May-mid-Sept. Tel. (0902) 92912/72107.*

AVONDALE HOUSE

County Wicklow

This house, of 18th-c. design, is a two-storey building that was the birthplace and family home of Charles Stewart Parnell, the great 19th-c. nationalist leader, the uncrowned "king" of Ireland. The large hall opens into the reception and dining rooms, both of which are filled with Parnell memorabilia. Much of the house has now been restored to its decor of around 1850. An audio-visual presentation on the life and times of Parnell precedes the tour of the house. Basement kitchen is now a tearoom. The surrounding forest estate extends to over 200 hectares (500 acres), and is a fine testimony to Ireland's natural heritage of trees, plants and animals. The oldest trees were planted by Samuel Hayes, who built the house over two centuries ago. *1.6 km (1 mile) S of Rathdrum. Admission charge. Open 11am-6pm daily, all year, except Christmas Day. Tel. (0404) 46111.*

BALLITORE QUAKER MUSEUM

Ballitore, County Kildare

The tiny village of Ballitore, a substantial Quaker settlement in the 18th c., has a Quaker museum in part of the old meeting house. A branch of the County Kildare library service has the ground floor. Quakers still meet there on Sundays. In 1994 the first Quaker wedding

to be held here in over a century took place. In the museum itself are Quaker relics, including a late 18th-c. wedding gown and bonnet, lace, tapestry and embroidery, plus documentation on the Quaker community. Ballitore was renowned for its school; among its pupils was the 18th c. philosopher, Edmund Burke. The village also has a Quaker burial ground. Nearby **Crookstown mill and heritage centre** is in a converted 1840 cornmill and details the baking and milling trades and local history. Willie Kelly, a local historian, conducts walking tours of this historic village by arrangement. He can be contacted through the museum.
30 km (18 miles) S of Naas, immediately off the N9 to Carlow.
Museum: *Admission charge. Open 9am-5pm Mon-Fri, all year, also 11am-5pm Sat, 2pm-5pm Sun, May-Sept. Tel. (0507) 23344.*
Mill: *Admission charge. Open 10am-7pm (5pm in winter) daily, all year. Tel. (0507) 23222.*

BALLYCASTLE MUSEUM

Ballycastle, County Antrim

The museum in this striking town on the north Antrim coast is located in what was once the courthouse and market hall dating from the 18th c. when Ballycastle was planned as an industrial town. Pioneering industries begun then included coal-mining and glass-making, but none lasted. Early this century, Ballycastle played its part in the Celtic revival and the museum has samples of this work. The most significant item is one of the original banners from the first Glens of Antrim *feis*, or festival, in 1904, together with sculptures, paintings, print and craftwork from this time. Among the artists represented is Stephen Clarke, once manager of the well-known Irish Home Industries shop in Ballycastle, An Tuirne Beag.
19 km (13 miles) E of Giant's Causeway. Admission free. Open 12noon-6pm Mon-Sat, end June-early Sept. Tel. (012657) 62225.

BALLYHACK CASTLE

Ballyhack, County Wexford

This Crusader castle was built about 1450 by the Knights Hospitaller of St John and has been partially restored. On the E shore of Waterford harbour, it looks over to Passage East in County Waterford; the two villages are connected by car ferry. The castle is one of about 3,500 tower houses built in Ireland between the 14th and 17th c. and Ballyhack castle is a particularly fine example. The first floor vaulted chamber is being developed to show the history of the Normans in Ireland. The original castle had six storeys. Among the features still existing are some of the original fireplaces, a chapel and dressing rooms, together with a cell in which prisoners were kept; the only entrance was through a narrow grill-covered opening high above the cell. Near the castle are the village's tourist office and the Neptune restaurant.

13 km (8 miles) E of Waterford city (via Passage East and car ferry). Admission charge. Open 12noon-6pm Wed-Sun, Apr, June, Sept, 10am-6pm daily, July, Aug, or by arr. Tel. (051) 389468/389164/389284.

BALLYMORE HISTORIC FEATURES

Camolin, County Wexford

This "walkabout" open-air museum has an intriguing range of interesting places, including a Norman motte, an ancient church, graveyard and holy well. The Donovan family have lived here for the past 300 years and describe this as a family museum. The large hayloft in the 18th c. farmyard buildings has been converted into an indoor museum and it has a very eclectic mixture that includes lace, embroidery, costumes, children's clothes, toys, a late 19th c. wedding dress and old farm accounts and records. In the adjoining former dairy, old dairy equipment and household items are on display, while horse-drawn farm equipment is also on show. Tearoom.

Ballymore, Camolin, 10 km (6 miles) SW of Gorey, off the N11 (signposted). Admission charge. Open 2pm-6pm Thurs-Sun, June-Sept, also Easter, bank holidays. Tel. (054) 83189.

BANDON HERITAGE CENTRE

Bandon, County Cork

The West Cork market town of Bandon has one of Ireland's oldest Protestant churches, Christ Church, originally built in 1610 (the oldest is reckoned to be St Patrick's Church of Ireland in Newry, built in 1575). Bandon was once a staunchly Protestant town, but Christ Church, long deconsecrated, now houses a heritage centre with a number of disparate themes. The distilling and brewing section recalls Allman's whiskey distillery in the town and includes some old bottles from the company. Another section, called O'Briens, features a traditional grocery store with wooden packaging and old advertisements, also a traditional country pub, complete with wooden counter and old bottles. The schoolroom faithfully recreates the old style of learning, with rows of wooden desks, a blackboard and even satchels hung up.

32 km (20 miles) SW of Cork city. Turn right at town bridge when approaching from Cork direction. Admission charge. Open 10am-6pm Mon-Sat, 2pm-6pm Sun, June-Oct. Tel. (023) 44193.

BANTRY HOUSE AND FRENCH ARMADA CENTRE

Bantry, County Cork

Bantry House, one of the finest 18th-c. stately homes in Ireland, has a fascinating interior, beginning with the inner hall. The Rose and Drawing Rooms have many fine furnishings, including 18th-c. Savonnerie carpets and Aubusson tapestries in the latter. The dining-room is lined with portraits, while the long library, complete with grand piano, looks out on the terraced Italian-style gardens. From the bedrooms at the front of the house, the views extend across Bantry Bay. The house is complemented by the new French Armada centre, commemorating the abortive French landings in Bantry Bay in 1796. Models of the ships that took part, old medals, lithographs and paintings, besides reconstructions of incidents, help tell the story in an attractive modern format. The centrepiece of the exhibition is the 1:6 scale model of the frigate

Surveillante, scuppered off Whiddy Island, while another depicts Wolfe Tone in his cabin.
3 km (2 miles) SW of Bantry town on N71 to Ballydehob. Admission charge. House open 9am-8pm daily in summer (6pm winter). Centre open 10am-6pm daily, all year. Tel. (027) 51796.

BATTLE OF AUGHRIM CENTRE

Aughrim, County Galway

Visitors can relive the day that changed Irish and European history, the battle fought in fog on 12 July 1691. A total of 45,000 soldiers from eight European countries came to fight; by nightfall some 9,000 had been slain. The victory of Williamite forces over Jacobite troops had profound effects on the course of European history, as had the Battle of the Boyne, fought a year earlier. Tearoom. Just outside the village, the actual battlefield is signposted.
6 km (3.5 miles) SW of Ballinasloe on N6. Admission charge. Open 10am-6pm daily, Easter-Sept, or by arr. Tel. (0905) 73939.

BELLEEK POTTERY

Belleek, County Fermanagh

The flamboyantly-decorated Parian ware made at Belleek, a tiny village in south-west Fermanagh, since 1857 has become world-renowned. At the pottery, visitors can see the production process for themselves, including the hand-crafting of the basketware designs that characterise Belleek and the hand-painting of the designs. The museum, with its classical-style columns, has many examples of Belleek pottery made since the pottery's foundation, including the earthenware which was produced for its first ten years. A presentation in the audio-visual theatre completes the tour. Shop, restaurant.
8 km (5 miles) E of Ballyshannon, County Donegal. Admission charge. Open 9am-6pm Mon-Fri, 10am-6pm Sat, 2pm-6pm Sun, Mar-Sept, 9am-5pm Mon-Fri, Oct-Feb. Pottery tours, weekdays, every 20 mins. Tel. (013656) 658501.

BERKELEY COSTUME AND TOY MUSEUM

New Ross, County Wexford

A collection of toys and costumes, nearly all made in Ireland, between about 1740 and 1925. Exhibits also include toy carriages and embroidered textiles. One of the most interesting pieces is a dress made in Kilkenny about 1760. The 18th c. costumes in particular are remarkably extravagant in their use of materials, colours and embroidery. Altogether there are hundreds of exhibits in the 18th-c. house, owned by the Bernstorff family. Many of the items are on display in the dining room and drawing room and children can go for a ride in the Victorian goat carriage in the garden.

6 km (4 miles) NE of New Ross, off the N79 to Enniscorthy (signposted). Admission charge. Open 2pm-7pm daily, May-Sept. Tel. (051) 21361.

BEWLEY'S MUSEUM

Dublin

Dublin and Bewley's, the chain of cafés founded in 1840, are inextricably linked. Locals and visitors alike still revel in the smell of roast coffee and the delights of the sticky bun in Bewley's cafés, especially at Grafton Street and Westmoreland Street. A small area on the first floor of the Grafton Street café, which once housed Bewley's chocolate factory, has been turned into a museum, with family portraits, old equipment, teapots from the 1920s and even an old one-penny lavatory lock.

Grafton Street, Dublin 2. Admission free. Open 9am-6pm Mon-Sat, all year. Tel. (01) 677 6761.

BLASKET CENTRE

Dunquin, County Kerry

This centre, with a modern under-stated design, commemorates the heritage of the nearby Blasket Islands. The islands had a strong cultural tradition, reflected in the creation of various literary masterpieces in Irish, and a distinctive way of life which endured until the last of the islanders abandoned their homes on Great Blasket Island in 1953. The new centre describes in detail the old island way of life, its social and literary traditions and the flora and fauna of the islands. The extensive research on the islands' history is available in the centre's library, which also has display areas and a room where the sounds of the islands are recreated (the Fuaim Room). Bookshop, restaurant.

25 km (15 miles) W of Dingle. Admission charge. Open 10am-6pm, daily, Easter-June, Sept, 10am-7pm daily, June-Aug. Tel. (066) 56444.

BOYLE, COUNTY ROSCOMMON

The small town of Boyle has three outstanding properties. The Cistercian **Boyle Abbey,** one of the best preserved in Ireland, founded in 1161 by monks from Mellifont abbey in County Louth, has substantial ruins including cloisters, church and sacristy; the chancel and the transepts, both 12th c., are the oldest part of the church. The gatehouse houses an interpretative centre. **Frybrook House,** in Boyle town centre, was built about 1750 as an elegant three-storey Georgian style house overlooking the Boyle river. The drawing room has some of the finest Georgian decorative plasterwork in Ireland.

King House, off Main Street, was built in the 18th c. for the King family and was later a barracks for the Connaught Rangers. The house has now been turned

Fireplace at King House, Boyle

into an interpretative centre, using 3D displays, audio-visual presentations and special effects to tell the history of Boyle and the King family, besides the turbulent pageantry of Connaught kings and chieftains, among them the O'Conors and the McDermotts.

40 km (25 miles) SE of Sligo on N4

Boyle abbey: *Admission charge. Open 9.30am-6.30pm daily, June-Sept.*

Frybrook House: *Admission charge. Open 2pm-6pm Tues-Sun, Apr-Sept. Tel. (079) 63033.*

King House: *Admission charge. Open 10am-6pm Tues-Sun, May-Sept, Sat, Sun, Oct-Apr. Tel. (079) 63242/26100.*

BRAY HERITAGE CENTRE

Bray, County Wicklow

Located in an old courthouse, built in 1841, but with a well modernised two-storey interior, this centre tells the story of Bray and its rise to prominence as a seaside resort. The arrival of the railway in the town in 1853 was the key element for change and there's plenty of detail about William Dargan (1799-1867), the railway pioneer, accompanied by a fine model of Bray railway station and old photographs. The building of the seafront esplanade from 1859 onwards is detailed, along with some of Bray's now-vanished buildings, including the Turkish Baths on the seafront. Bray's tourist information office is located here.

Lower Main Street, beside Royal Hotel. Admission charge. Open 10am-5pm daily, all year. Tel. (01) 286 6716/286 7128.

BRONTË HOMELAND INTERPRETATIVE CENTRE

near Rathfriland, County Down

Patrick Brontë, father of Charlotte, Emily and Anne, the famous Brontë sisters, was born near Rathfriland, County Down, in 1777. The story of the Brontë family is told at Drumballyroney church and schoolhouse, where Patrick first preached and where he taught. The centre includes displays on the Brontë family's history and connections with the area, complete with

photographs and models. After seeing the centre, visitors can go on a tour of nearby sites connected with the Brontë family, including the remains of Patrick's birthplace cottage at Emdale, the site of the school where he taught at Glascar, and the cottage where his mother, Alice McClory, was brought up. The picnic site at Knockiveagh gives excellent views of the surrounding hills and landscapes where Patrick Brontë grew up.
Drumballyroney church and school are 5 km (3 miles) NE of Rathfriland. Admission charge. Open 11am-5pm Tues-Fri, 2pm-6pm Sat, Sun, Mar-Oct. Tel. (018206) 31152.

BUNRATTY, COUNTY CLARE
The many aspects of this world-famous **folk park** deserve a full day's exploration, taking in the many 18th- and 19th-c. buildings that have been reconstructed here with complete authenticity. They include eight farmhouses, a watermill and a blacksmith's forge. A complete village street has been recreated, with all manner of shops, from an old-style printers to a pub, post office, even a school. The interiors of all the

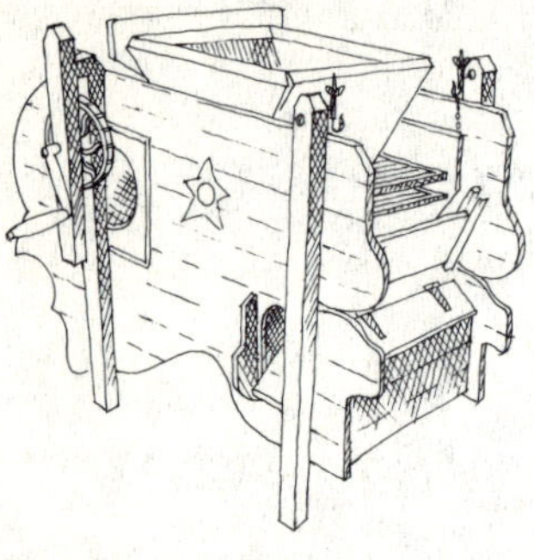

Winnowing machine, Bunratty Folk Park

buildings have antique furniture and artefacts, giving a good insight into the way of life of previous generations. If you walk through the folk village to the courtyard of Bunratty House, you'll come to the collection of old agricultural machinery. Also at the back of the park is the **Bunratty Winery Museum,** where exhibits include everything from fossils to a poitín still. Conclude the tour at **Bunratty Castle,** at the entrance to the folk park: built in 1425, its medieval splendour, complete with furnishings and tapestries, was restored in the 1950s. Restaurants, shops.

13 km (8 miles) W of Limerick on N18 to Shannon airport.

Folk park and castle: *Admission charge. Open 9.30am-7pm daily, July, Aug (closes 5.30pm for rest of year). Tel. (061) 361511.*

Bunratty winery museum: *Admission free. Open 10am-5.30pm daily, all year. Tel. (061) 362222.*

BURREN DISPLAY CENTRE

Kilfenora, County Clare

A fine introduction to the flora and fauna of the Burren, this centre has displays showing the archaeology, history, local treasures and unique flowers of the district, together with a large-scale model of the Burren landscape. Audio-visual presentation.

Poulnabrone dolmen, the Burren

Craft shop. Next to the centre are the substantial ruins of a 12th-c. cathedral. Also in County Clare, the **Corofin Heritage Centre,** in a converted church, has a small but comprehensive museum on life in 19th-c. Clare. The nearby **Dysert O'Dea castle** has an archaeology centre, with local museum and audio-visual presentation.

Burren display centre: *Kilfenora, 11 km (7 miles) SE of Lisdoonvarna. Admission charge. Open 10am-5pm daily, Mar, Apr, Sept, Oct, 9.30am-6pm daily, May-Aug. Tel. (065) 88030.*

Corofin heritage centre: *15 km (8 miles) N of Ennis. Admission charge. Open 10am-6pm daily, Easter-Oct. Tel. (065) 37955.*

Dysert O'Dea castle: *3 km (2 miles) S of Corofin. Admission charge. Open 10am-7pm daily, May-Sept. Tel. (065) 27722.*

BURREN HERITAGE CENTRE

near Warrenpoint, County Down

Not to be confused with the Burren in County Clare, this converted national school, sited at the foot of the Mountains of Mourne, uses interpretative models, exhibitions and audio-visual aids to tell the story of the locality. In the main exhibition hall are models of prehistoric sites in the area and Neolithic tools. Many 18th- and 19th-c. artefacts recall social history. Exhibitions, lectures, gift and book shop, café. Also worth seeing in the area is the **Mullaghbawn Folk Museum** in the Ring of Gullion in south Armagh. The two-roomed thatched cottage highlights the local history, landscape and wildlife.

Burren heritage centre: *3 km (2 miles) inland from turn-off midway between Narrow Water Castle and Warrenpoint (signposted). Admission charge. Open 11am-6pm Tues-Sat, 2pm-6pm Sun, Apr-Sept, 10am-5pm Mon-Fri, Oct-Mar. Tel. (016937) 73378.*

Mullaghbawn Folk Museum: *20 km (12 miles) SW of Newry. Take A25 towards Bessbrook, then the B30 (signposted). Admission charge. Open 11am-7pm daily, May-Sept, 2pm-6pm Sun, Oct-Apr. Tel. (01693) 888785/ 888108.*

BUSHMILLS DISTILLERY

Bushmills, County Antrim

The world's oldest distillery, still working, can trace its origins back to 1276. Its original grant to distil was made in 1608. This great pedigree is fully reflected in the whiskies produced, including Bushmills Malt, Black Bush and the standard Bushmills, itself aged for up to seven years. The visitor centre consists of the Potstill bar and two shops. In the bar can be seen the old malt kilns, once used for drying the malt.

12 km (8 miles) N of Coleraine. Admission charge. Open 9am-12noon, 1.30pm-3.30pm Mon-Thurs, 9am-12noon, Fri, Sept-May, until 4pm Mon-Fri, 10am-4pm Sat, June-Aug. Tel. (012657) 31521.

CAPE CLEAR ISLAND MUSEUM

Cape Clear, County Cork

The island, measuring 5x3 km (3x2 miles), is 11 km (7 miles) off the West Cork coast. It has a wealth of folklore tradition, a resident population of 135 that increases to about 700 in summer and is Irish-speaking. The many facets of this diverse island life can be seen in the museum, housed in a former schoolhouse. Few parishes anywhere in Ireland can claim such an assiduous collection of local material, which includes household items such as a dresser from an island kitchen. Cape Clear's rich fishing tradition is recalled, along with the numerous shipwrecks in the area. Material from some of those wrecks, everything from delph to saloon doors, is on display. Fishing is the island's main economic activity and is reflected in the museum's contents. More history can be seen in the island's three pubs, including Paddy Burke's bar, which has remained virtually unchanged in the past century.

Ferries from Baltimore and Schull. Admission charge. Open 2pm-5.30pm daily, June-Aug, or by arr. Tel. (028) 39119/(021) 893638.

CARLINGFORD VISITOR CENTRE

Carlingford, County Louth

Carlingford town, set enticingly on the Cooley

peninsula on the S shores of Carlingford Lough has been much restored in recent years. Historic medieval buildings include the imposing ruins of King John's castle, the Mint and the Tholsel. Taaffe's Castle, a 15th c. square tower, is also now being restored. The historical glories of the town are recaptured in the Holy Trinity cultural and visitor centre in a restored Church of Ireland church.
25 km (15 miles) NE of Dundalk. Admission charge. Open 9.30am-5pm daily, May-Aug, Sat, Sun, Mar, Apr, Sept, Oct, Nov-Mar, by arr. Tel. (042) 73454.

CARRICK-ON-SUIR, COUNTY TIPPERARY
This historic town has two interesting sites, Ormond Castle at the E end of the Main Street and the town's heritage centre at the W end of the same street. **Ormond Castle** is a 16th c. Elizabethan manor house, now finely restored. It was built about 1564-68 by the 10th Earl of Ormond to receive his cousin, Queen Elizabeth I, who in the event never came to Ireland.

Ormond Castle, Carrick-on-Suir

The **heritage centre,** in a former Church of Ireland church, has many relics of life in old Carrick, everything from slate and chalk once used in a local school, to old grocery bills and old photographs. A stock and apprentices wage book, used by Stephenson Bros drapery shop in the town in 1846 is on display, along with willow baskets made by Joe Shanahan in the town about 1880.

Ormond Castle: *Admission charge. Open 9.30am-6.30pm daily, June-Sept. Tel. (051) 640787.*
Heritage centre: *Admission charge. Open 9am-5pm Mon-Fri, all year, also 2.30pm-5.30pm Sat, Sun, summer. Tel. (051) 640200.*

CARRIGLAS MANOR

near Longford, County Longford

This Gothic Revival house has been the home of the Lefroy family, of Huguenot descent, since it was built in 1837. In keeping with its period, it is romantically, castellated and turreted. The interior has fine ceilings, pictures, furniture and other artefacts, while the stableyard, built by the architect James Gandon (who was also responsible for the Custom House in Dublin) about 1790, is the only remaining example of his agricultural work. The walled garden has been restored. Gift shop, tearoom.
5 km (3 miles) NE of Longford on the R194 to Granard. Admission charge. Open 1.30pm-6pm daily except Tues, Wed, June-Sept, or by arr. Tel. (043) 45165.

CARROTHERS FAMILY MUSEUM

Lisbellaw, County Fermanagh

This family-run collection has an informality that cannot exist in larger museums. In the best family tradition, it has a little bit of everything, including farming and household utensils, as well as mementoes of family life going back 200 years. The museum has much 19th c. documentation including wages books and deeds, besides letters written home by members of the family who emigrated to North America and from the front in World War I.
11 km (7 miles) SE of Enniskillen on A4 to Lisnaskea. Admission charge. Open daily by arr. Tel. (01365) 387278.

CASHEL, COUNTY TIPPERARY

This historic town, dominated by the **Rock of Cashel,** has several points of interest, not least the Rock itself, with its medieval ecclesiastical buildings dating back to the 12th c. The entrance to the Rock is through the Hall of the Vicars Choral, where an audio-visual presentation, *Strongholds of Faith*, is shown. There is also a small museum in this hall. The most striking part of the ruins is the cathedral, much of which dates from the 13th c.

Cashel also has a new **heritage centre,** located in the Town Hall on Main Street. Its highlight is a model of the town as it was in the 1640s. Other features of the town and surroundings are detailed, including the 8th and 9th c. Derrynaflan Hoard and the abbeys of County Tipperary. **Cashel Folk Village,** nearby, is a museum of rural life with an old style living-room, pub, butcher's shop (complete with ancient saws) and an old blacksmith's forge, complete with tools and bellows. Also worth seeing is the 18th c. Church of Ireland cathedral, and in its grounds, the **Bolton Library,** which has 12,000 books. It has many examples of early Irish printing, notably from the 17th c.

Rock of Cashel: *Admission charge. Open 9.30am-5.30pm daily, mid-Mar-mid-June, 9am-7.30pm daily, mid-June-mid-Sept, 9.30am-4.30pm daily, mid-Sept-mid-Mar. Tel. (062) 61437.*

Cashel Heritage Centre: *Admission charge. Open 10am-6pm daily, all year. Tel. (062) 61133.*

Folk Village: *Admission charge. Open 10am-7.30pm daily, all year. Tel. (062) 62525.*

Bolton Library: *Admission charge. Open by arr. Tel. (062) 61944.*

CASTLE MATRIX

Rathkeale, County Limerick

This early 15th-c. fortress tower (27 metres/90 ft high) has an extraordinary history. It was built on the banks of the River Deel, a tributary of the River Shannon, by the fourth and seventh Earls of Desmond, a father and son. They had a fine library here and were renowned for their knowledge of ancient history and religion. In the early 19th c., linen was being made here, while there was also a flour mill and a sawmill. During the 1930s, the castle was abandoned and fell into ruin before being bought and rescued in the early 1960s by Colonel Sean O'Driscoll of the US Air Force. He spent the last 30 years of his life restoring it and building his collection of books, art and artefacts from around the world.

27 km (17 miles) SW of Limerick on N20. Admission charge. Tours of castle 11am-5pm daily, May-Sept, or by arr. Tel. (069) 64284.

CASTLETOWN HOUSE

Celbridge, County Kildare

Ireland's largest and finest Palladian country house was built about 1722 for William Conolly, a lawyer who was not only the Speaker of the Irish House of Commons but, by the time the house was built, the wealthiest man in Ireland. The structure of the house is being extensively refurbished, although work on the West Wing is unlikely to be completed until about 1997. The house remains open to visitors. The first set piece encountered is the magnificent two-storey entrance hall, decorated with white plasterwork. On the ground floor, a series of grand rooms lead one into the next, among them the brown study and red and green drawing-rooms, all with authentic 18th c. furniture, fittings and wallpaper. The great staircase leads to the first floor, where the Long Gallery runs the whole length of the building, magnificently decorated in the Pompeian style, with wall paintings and three glass chandeliers made in Venice. From the windows of the Long Gallery can be seen the Conolly Folly, 3 km (2 miles) distant, built to create employment in the harsh winter of 1739. Coffee shop.

24 km (15 miles) W of Dublin. The entrance to Castletown park is at the end of Celbridge's Main Street. Admission charge. Open 10am-6pm Mon-Fri, 11am-6pm Sat, 2pm-6pm Sun, Apr-Sept, 10am-5pm Mon-Fri, 2pm-5pm Sun, bank holidays, Oct, 2pm-5pm Sun, bank holidays Nov-Mar. Tel. (01) 628 8252.

CÉIDE FIELDS VISITOR CENTRE

County Mayo

The Céide Fields centre, looking like a modern pyramid, stands overlooking spectacular cliffs on the north Mayo coast. The story it tells, of the Stone Age landscapes preserved beneath the blanket bogs of this part of Mayo, is equally dramatic. The life of this Stone Age farming community, with its stone-walled fields, homes and megalithic tombs, together with their craft skills and spiritual beliefs, is recreated inside the centre, which is dominated by a 5,000-year-old Scots pine tree. Viewing platforms inside and outside the glass-topped pyramid give striking views over land and sea.

8 km (5 miles) W of Ballycastle on the R314 Ballycastle-Belmullet road. Admission charge. Open 10am-5pm daily, mid-Mar-May, Oct, 9.30am-6.30pm daily, June-Sept, 10am-4.30pm daily, Nov, winter by arr. Tel. (096) 43325.

CÉIM HILL MUSEUM

Union Hall, County Cork

This West Cork museum is unique in that it's a one person collection, reflecting the many local history interests of Therese O'Mahony. She describes the museum as telling the story of her townland from the time of the dinosaurs to her own period and the collection even boasts some fossilised dinosaur droppings! Jawbones and teeth that once belonged to an Irish elk nestle side by side with more recent exhibits, including a soup pot from the famine era, old farm implements, items from the War of Independence and local historical costumes. The location of the museum is quite spectacular, overlooking Castletownshend and its estuary.

15 km (9 miles) SW of Rosscarbery (signposted). Admission charge. Open daily, by arr. Tel. (028) 36280.

CIVIC MUSEUM

Dublin

One of this small museum's claims to fame is the head of Lord Nelson, from the O'Connell Street statue blown up in 1966. Once the city's Assembly House,

the museum, run by Dublin Corporation, has frequent and interesting exhibitions on many aspects of Dublin life, despite its lack of size. The planned refurbishment of **City Hall** by the Corporation is due to include an interpretative centre for displaying Dublin's civic regalia.
South William Street, beside Powerscourt Town House centre. Admission free. Open 10am-5pm Tues-Sat, 2pm-5pm Sun, all year. Tel. (01) 679 4260.
City Hall: *Dame Street, Dublin 2. Admission free. Open 9am-5.30pm Mon-Fri, all year. Tel. (01) 679 6111.*

CLONAKILTY, COUNTY CORK

The **Model Village,** set overlooking the estuary, depicts in miniature form the West Cork railway which closed down, amidst much chagrin, over 30 years ago, and the main towns of the region. A highlight of the village are the models of Clonakilty houses painted in bright Mediterranean colours. The village is due to be completed by 1996, when it will feature many other aspects of West Cork life in miniature, including the unique fishing vessels that used to ply these waters. Also in Clonakilty, the **West Cork regional museum,** in a former schoolhouse, has memorabilia relating to Michael Collins, records from Clonakilty Corporation dating back to 1675 and material on the local post office. At Ballinascarthy, 8 km (5 miles) NE of the town on the N71 to Bandon, the **Lisselan estate** has a marker showing the site of the old Ford homestead, where William Ford, father of Henry Ford, the motor pioneer, was born and brought up. A replica homestead and a Ford museum are planned.
Clonakilty is 53 km (33 miles) SW of Cork.
Model village: *Admission charge. Open 11am-5pm daily, all year. Tel. (023) 33224.*
West Cork regional museum: *Admission charge. Open 10.30am-5.30pm Mon-Sat, 3pm-5pm Sun, May-Oct.*
Lisselan estate: *Tel. (023) 33249.*

COBH, COUNTY CORK

This seaside town, developed in the 19th c. was once

the main emigration port for people sailing to North America. The story of that relentless emigration is told in the fine **Queenstown Story** centre. Using audio-visual techniques, artefacts and models, the centre recreates emigration history and recalls the appalling conditions on the aptly-named coffin ships that crossed the Atlantic. Conditions aboard the convict ships that went to Australia is also detailed while, more genteelly, the centre tells the story of the great ocean

Sirius, *Cobh heritage centre*

liners that once called at Cobh. Among them were the *Titanic,* which sank in 1912, and the *Lusitania,* torpedoed off the Old Head of Kinsale in 1915. In the Old Church cemetery, 2 km (1 mile) N of the town, many victims of the *Lusitania* sinking are buried.

Also in Cobh, the former Presbyterian church, known as the **Scots Church,** was opened as a museum in 1973. It too has many interesting artefacts from former industries, including the Belvelly Brickworks. Models of Cork harbour coasters, marine paintings and maritime photographs are also in the collection.

24 km (15 miles) SE of Cork city.

Queenstown Story: *Admission charge. Open 10am-6pm daily, Feb-Dec. Tel. (021) 813591.*

Scots Church Museum: *Admission charge. Open 11am-1pm, 2pm-6pm daily, Apr-Sept, 3pm-6pm Sun, all year. Tel. (021) 811555/811260.*

COIS ABHAINN FOLK MUSEUM

Corraun Peninsula, County Mayo

This small museum, on the Corraun peninsula, near Achill Sound, is in a three-room cottage that dates back 120 years; it has been extensively restored. The kitchen includes an open fireplace complete with utensils and a settle bed, while old photographs recall people and places on the island; tragedies too, including one in 1937 when migrant workers from the island died in a fire in a bothy in Kirkintilloch, Scotland.

3 km (2 miles) E of Achill Sound. Turn just before bridge to island (signposted). Admission charge. Open 10am-7pm daily, July-Sept. Tel. (098) 45178.

ST CONAL'S MUSEUM

Glenties, County Donegal

This museum, named after the saint who brought Christianity to west Donegal in the 6th c., is housed in two buildings. The older one is the 1843 courthouse (still used as such once a month), while a modern building was opened in 1994. There's a good collection of artefacts from the narrow gauge County Donegal Railways, including many old photographs and posters. Noted writers from the North-West, including Brian Friel and Patrick McGill are commemorated.

On Ardara road. Admission charge. Open 10am-1pm, 2pm-5pm Mon-Fri, 10.30am-12.30pm Sat, May-Sept, or by arr. Tel. (075) 51277.

COOLAKAY HOUSE AGRICULTURAL MUSEUM

Enniskerry, County Wicklow

This collection of agricultural implements and equipment is exhibited in a large shed divided into three sections and attached to Coolakay House. Items of old farming equipment include an early Ferguson tractor, a 1936 threshing machine, made in Aberdeen, Scotland, which travelled from farm to farm during the harvest, and an old combine harvester. Smaller items include a drill grubber, made by Pierces of Wexford, old hay rakes and ancient ploughs. The museum has a couple of tub traps and an old side cart. Restaurant. *4 km (3 miles) SW of Enniskerry (signposted). Open 10am-6pm daily, all year. Tel. (01) 286 2423.*

CORK CITY GAOL AND BROADCASTING MUSEUM

This jail received its first prisoners in 1824 and was last used as such in 1923. This magnificent architectural set piece languished in dereliction until it was reopened as a visitor attraction in 1993. The west wing, with cells on three floors, has been thoroughly and convincingly restored. A spectacular multi-media presentation depicts Cork social history in the 19th c., explaining why so many people in the city were driven to crime. The penal regime they encountered is well documented, including the infamous Cork treadwheel, while the governor and his office have also been recreated in lifesize model form. When the first Cork radio station was set up in 1927, the top floor of the governor's house was used for studios, and this same floor is now planned to house RTE's broadcasting museum. It will trace the history of radio and television in Ireland. Broadcasting artefacts and details of noted presenters and performers will be designed for general and special interest visitors. Café, craft and bookshop.

Sunday's Well, N bank of River Lee, opposite Fitzgerald's Park and Western Road (signposted). Admission charge. Open 9.30am-6pm daily, Mar-Oct, tours at 10.30am, 2.30pm Mon-Fri, 10am-5pm Sat, Sun, Nov-Feb. Tel. (021) 305022.

NB Cork Broadcasting Museum on line to open in 1996.

CORK HERITAGE PARK

Cork City

This new centre is most attractively set in a 3 ha (7 acre) park. It is part of a great estate that once belonged to the Pike family, Quakers who played a prominent part in Cork business life in the 18th and 19th c. A central point of interest in the park is the bell tower that once stood atop the Beamish and Crawford brewery in

South Main Street, Cork, to summon the workers. The Pikes' Bessboro house is now owned by a religious order, but the courtyard, once the servants' quarters, has been converted into a series of themed exhibition areas.

The history of the port of Cork is detailed, with a large model of the whole port area made by the Cork Harbour Commissioners in 1932, restored and updated. Many other maritime relics include photographs of Cork harbour around 1890, ships' models (the Pike family originally set up the Cork Steam Packet Company) and the free pass given by that company to Winston Churchill in 1922.

A key feature of the centre is the elaborate section on fire brigades; it is reckoned to be the only fire service museum in Ireland. Fire fighting is traced back to the 18th c. when insurance companies ran primitive fire brigades (only for those who had paid their premiums) through to early breathing apparatus. The burning of Cork in 1920 by the Black and Tans is recalled. Café.
Bessboro, Blackrock, SE Cork city. Approach through Douglas (signposted). Admission charge. Open 10.30am-5pm daily, all year. Tel. (021) 358854.

CORK PUBLIC MUSEUM
Cork City
Founded in 1945, the city museum, set in Fitzgerald Park by the River Lee, is very much a traditional style museum, but well maintained and presented. Beside its entrance is the coat of arms, carved in stone, of the City of Cork, rescued after City Hall was burned by the Black and Tans in 1920. Inside, rooms display the prehistory of the Cork region, details on the War of Independence and many examples of Cork crafts. These include 18th-c. silver, now much prized, besides the even rarer Republican silver, assayed in Cork in 1922, when times were too troubled for it to be sent to the Assay Office in Dublin. Cork glassware and Youghal needlepoint lace are also featured.
Fitzgerald Park, off Western Road (signposted). Admission free. Open 11am-1pm, 2.15pm-5pm Mon-Fri, Sept-May (6pm June, July, Aug), 3pm-5pm Sun, all year. Tel. (021) 270679.

CORLEA TRACKWAY CENTRE

Keenagh, County Longford

This new, futuristic interpretative centre built in the middle of the bogs displays the remnants of the prehistoric trackways that were laid through these bogs. In 1984 a trackway made of oak planks was discovered here, quickly followed by other similar wooden roads. Samples of the wood were calculated to date from the fourth millenium BC. In all, over 50 of these prehistoric superhighways were discovered in the area and their history and relevance is well documented here. Twenty metres (65 ft) of trackway is on display in the centre; visitors can even see the marks of the tools used to cut the wood.

15 km (9 miles) S of Longford on R397 to Keenagh village. In the village, take signposted turn to the centre, a further 3 km (2 miles). Admission charge. Open 9.30am-6.30pm daily, June-Sept. Tel. (043) 22386.

CORNMILL HERITAGE CENTRE

Coalisland, County Tyrone

Coalisland was at the heart of the original industrial revolution in the North of Ireland and its history is related in this new centre located in a renovated early 20th c. corn mill. Many facets of the town's industrial history are recorded, including coal-mining, developed nearly two centuries ago, after coal was discovered in the adjacent district of Congo. The town had a short-lived coal-mining rush, iron-making was also practised and a canal was dug to nearby Lough Neagh. The audio-visual presentation, in the theatre on the top floor of the centre, uses recorded folk memories.

6 km (4 miles) NE of Dungannon. Admission charge. Open 10am-6pm Mon-Fri, Oct-May, 10am-8pm Mon-Fri, 11am-6pm Sat, 2pm-6pm Sun, June-Sept. Tel. (01868) 748532.

CROOM HERITAGE CENTRE

Croom, County Limerick

Set in a flour mill, which was built in 1788 and closed down in the late 1940s, this centre depicts the story

of the family who ran the mill and the milling techniques that they used. For 150 years, the mill with its waterwheel was the economic pivot of this small, attractive village. Visitors can also see a short audio-visual presentation. Craft shop, restaurant.
10 km (6 miles) SE of Adare. Admission charge. Open 9am-6pm daily, all year. Tel. (061) 397130.

CROSSMOLINA HERITAGE CENTRE

Crossmolina, County Mayo

This intriguing centre, opened in 1992, has a fine collection of vintage farm implements, all dating from the horse-drawn era. Woodcutting is featured, with an original saw pit in operation. Visitors can also see the Mayo spade, or gowl-gob, a two-pronged instrument exclusive to this locality. Regular demonstrations of traditional crafts are given at the centre, which also features restored farm buildings and household utensils.
16 km (10 miles) W of Ballina. Admission charge. Open 10am-6pm Mon-Fri, all year, also 2pm-6pm Sat, Sun, June-Aug. Also by arr. Tel. (096) 31809.

CUSTOM HOUSE

Dublin

The Custom House, beside the River Liffey in central Dublin, is one of Ireland's great architectural masterpieces, designed by James Gandon and completed in 1791. Recently, the façade's shining white stonework has been well restored, and from 1996 visitors will be able to see the interior of the building for the first time.
Custom House Quay, Dublin 1. Admission free. Open 9am-5pm Mon-Fri, all year. Tel. (01) 679 3377.

MICHAEL DAVITT MUSEUM

Straide, County Mayo

Michael Davitt (1846-1906) was born, evicted and ultimately buried in Straide; his family eviction experiences helped shape his political convictions. He played a crucial role in pressing for the reform of

Ireland's land system, changing tenant farmers into owner occupiers. His life and works are recollected through the extensive collection of documents, photographs, prison and police records, letters, postcards, posters and personal possessions of the man. *15 km (9 miles) NW of Castlebar on N5/N58. Admission charge. Open 10am-6pm daily, Apr-Oct. Tel. (094) 56488/31022.*

DERRYNANE, NEAR CAHERDANIEL, COUNTY KERRY

Derrynane House and estate, once the home of Daniel O'Connell, the "Liberator" responsible for Catholic Emancipation in Ireland in the 19th c., is now a place of reverential remembrance. The house itself is most attractive, with its slate-faced exterior, while the interior is surprisingly homely and comforting for a grand house. The dining- and drawing-rooms are packed with furniture, paintings and other mementoes relating to O'Connell, including a table decorated with carvings of Irish wolfhounds and a harp presented to him by Dublin Corporation when he was an alderman of that city. The centrepiece of the museum is O'Connell's grand and elaborate ceremonial coach, which had lain forgotten for a century and has now been magnificently restored. The story of the great man and his works is narrated in an audio-visual presentation. The surrounding national park extends for 121 ha (298 acres). Café.
2 km (1 mile) W of Caherdaniel on the N70 Ring-of-Kerry road. Admission charge. Open 1pm-5pm Tues-Sun, Mar, Apr, Oct, 9am-6pm Mon-Sat, 11am-7pm Sun, May-Sept, 1pm-5pm Sat, Sun, Nov-Feb, or by arr. Tel. (066) 75113.

DE VALERA MUSEUM

Bruree, County Limerick

Eamon de Valera (1882-1975) was one of modern Ireland's great political leaders. Brought up in this small village on the banks of the River Maigue, the schoolhouse where he attended is now a museum. The desk with his initials carved in it has a place of honour.

10 km (6.5 miles) NW of Kilmallock. Admission charge. Open 9am-4.30pm Tues-Fri, 2.30pm-5.30pm Sat, Sun, all year, or by arr. Tel. (063) 91300.

DOUGLAS HYDE CENTRE

Frenchpark, County Roscommon

Dr Douglas Hyde was Ireland's first President and this permanent exhibition on his life and work is housed in the former Church of Ireland church at Portahard, where his father was once rector. Dr Hyde was a prominent scholar and his collection of prose and poetry can be seen here, along with such personal items as his gavel and walking stick. The centre has also the letter nominating him as President in 1938. Outside, the Gairdín an Chraoibhín (Garden of the Little Branch) has trees and shrubs that are sacred in Celtic mythology. Douglas Hyde's grave is at the rear of the church.

25 km (15 miles) NW of Strokestown on the N5. Admission charge. Open 2pm-5pm Tues-Fri, 2pm-6pm Sat, Sun, May-Sept, or by arr. Tel. (0907) 70016.

DOWN COUNTY MUSEUM

Downpatrick, County Down

The museum, opened in 1984, is in the old Down County gaol, built between 1789 and 1796, the most complete surviving Irish gaol of its period. The gatehouses of the museum are occupied by the St Patrick heritage centre, which tells the story of Ireland's patron saint through large-scale illustrations. Saint Patrick is reputedly buried in the graveyard of nearby Down cathedral, while just 3 km (2 miles) distant is the reputed site of his first church at Saul. More material on Saint Patrick is planned for the heritage centre. In the centre of the gaol site, surrounded by high walls, is the former governor's residence, which now houses the main museum galleries. Shop, tearoom.

The Mall, Downpatrick. Admission free. Open 11am-5pm Tues-Fri, 2pm-5pm Sat, all year, also open 2pm-5pm Sun, 11am-5pm Mon, July-mid-Sept. Tel. (01396) 615218.

DROMOD RAILWAY HERITAGE CENTRE

Dromod, County Leitrim

The Cavan and Leitrim narrow gauge railway opened in 1887 and closed in 1958. It ran from Dromod, on the main Dublin-Sligo line, to Belturbet in County Cavan, with a branch from Ballinamore to Drumshanbo and Arigna coal mines. Fondly remembered even today, the railway was as renowned in its day as the West Clare railway and, in the first stage of restoration, the laying of 0.8 km (0.5 mile) of track, rails that originally came from the West Clare railway were used. The plan is to extend the line for a further 8 km (5 miles) to Mohill. The old Cavan and Leitrim railway was slow but sure, with a maximum speed of 19 km (12 miles) per hour. The original station at Dromod, complete with ticket office and waiting room, has been restored, as have been the engine shed and water tower. Many relics of the line still exist, including hundreds of photographs taken during the 1950s by an English railway enthusiast, Michael Davies.

20 km (12 miles) NW of Longford. Admission charge. Open 1pm-6pm daily during summer or by arr. Tel. (078) 38599.

DUBLIN CASTLE

Dublin City

Originally built in the 13th c. on a Viking site, the castle served as a military fortress, prison, courts of law and centre of British administration in Ireland for 700 years. Extensive rebuilding took place in the 17th, 18th, 19th and 20th centuries and is continuing with the construction of new galleries that will house the Chester Beatty Library and Gallery of Oriental Art, planned to open here in 1997. Visitors can see the State Apartments, which include the grand staircase leading up to the Battleaxe Landing. Also open to visitors is the Church of the Most Holy Trinity, designed by Francis Johnston, architect of the GPO. The Company of Goldsmiths, the last remaining medieval guild in the city, is housed in the Dublin Castle complex and has interesting memorabilia, including paintings and documents. Dublin Castle has a gift shop and restaurant.

Off Dame Street, Dublin 2. Admission charge. Open

10am-12.15pm, 2pm-5pm Mon-Fri, 2pm-5pm Sat, Sun, bank holidays, Oct-June, 10am-5pm Mon-Fri, 2pm-5pm Sat, Sun, bank holidays, July-Sept. Tel. (01) 677 7129. Company of Goldsmiths, by arr only. Tel. (01) 475 1286.

DUBLINIA

Dublin City

Between 1875 and 1983, Irish bishops gathered in the Church of Ireland Synod Hall beside Christ Church cathedral. Now that building houses the Dublinia heritage centre which depicts life in medieval Dublin from 1170 to the closure of the monasteries in 1540. The entrance to the exhibition area features such topics as the Black Death plague, the languages used in medieval Dublin and the building of Dublin Castle. Some of the models are decidedly life like, especially that of the plague sufferer, while the background audio of old Dublin sounds is also realistic. Lifesize reconstructions include a merchant's house, with a leather-worker outside making shoes, and a quayside setting.

More Dublin history, 1,000 years of it, can be seen in the elaborate audio-visual presentation in Trinity College, the **Dublin Experience.**

Dublinia: *Beside Christ Church cathedral. Admission charge. Open 10am-5pm daily, Apr-Sept, 11am-4pm Mon-Sat, 10am-4.30pm Sun, Oct-Mar. Tel. (01) 679 4611.*

The Dublin Experience: *Thomas Davis Theatre, Arts Building, Trinity College. Admission charge. Open 10am-5pm daily, May-Oct. Shows every hour on the hour. Tel. (01) 677 2941.*

DUBLIN CITY LIBRARIES

Dublin has a remarkable collection of libraries and archives, enough material to satisfy any search for information. Dublin Corporation **city archives,** located in the civic museum offer access to considerable material about Dublin. The archives' stock includes a complete set of Thom's directories on the city from 1846 to the present and Wilson's directory, the predecessor to Thom's, begun in the 18th c. The **Irish Architectural Archive** has books, newspaper and magazine clippings on Ireland's architectural heritage, not just the golden Georgian era of the 18th c., but right up to present times. **Marsh's Library,** near St Patrick's cathedral, was built in the early 18th c. as the first public library in Ireland and has a collection of 25,000 books, many of them rare. Marsh's also has an interesting conservation section. The **National Library** has many first editions of work by Irish writers, practically every book ever published in Ireland and almost every newspaper and magazine. Themed exhibitions are staged here. The **National Archive** has many State papers and documents. **Pearse Street library** has a wealth of printed information on Dublin history and the Gilbert Collection of 18th c. books on the city.

The **Royal Irish Academy,** whose elegant building near the Mansion House has been thoroughly refurbished, has many rare medieval manuscripts and other early Irish material. **Trinity College** has two main libraries, the old and the new; the Long Room in the early-18th-c. library is the most impressive. Its most famous treasure, the Book of Kells, is on show in the Colonnades Gallery beneath the Long Room.

City Archives: *Civic Museum, South William Street, Dublin 2. Admission free. Open 10am-5pm Mon-Fri, by arr only. Museum closed Mon. Tel. (01) 677 5877.*

Irish Architectural Archive: *73 Merrion Square, Dublin 2. Admission charge. Open 10am-1pm, 2.30pm-5pm Tues-Fri, Sept-July. Tel.(01) 676 3430.*

Marsh's Library: *St Patrick's Close, Dublin 8. Admission donation. Open 10am-12.45pm, 2pm-5pm Mon, Wed, Thurs, Fri. 10.30am-1pm Sat, all year. Tel. (01) 454 3511.*

National Archive: *Bishop Street, Dublin 8. Admission free. Open 10am-5pm Mon-Fri, all year. Tel. (01) 478 3711.*

National Library: *Kildare Street, Dublin 2. Admission free. Open 10am-9pm Mon, 2pm-9pm Tues, Wed, 10am-5pm Thurs, Fri, 10am-1pm Sat, all year. Tel. (01) 661 8811.*

Pearse Street Library: *Dublin 2. Admission free. Open 10am-1pm, 2.15pm-5.30pm Mon-Thurs (5pm, Fri), 10am-1pm, 1.45pm-4.30pm Sat, all year. Tel. (01) 677 7662.*

Royal Irish Academy: *Dawson Street, Dublin 2. Admission free. Open 9.30am-5.30pm Mon-Fri, all year. Tel. (01) 676 2570.*

Trinity College: *Dublin 2. Admission charge. Open*

9.30am-5.30pm Mon-Sat, 12noon-5pm Sun, all year. Tel. (01) 677 2941.

DUNBRODY ABBEY

near Campile, County Wexford

Substantial ruins still exist of this Cistercian foundation, dating from around 1200 and founded by monks from St Mary's Abbey in Dublin. The site has a small museum, while a full-sized hedge maze is being developed, one of only two in Ireland. Crafts gallery, tearooms.

13 km (8 miles) S of New Ross. Admission charge. Open 10am-6pm daily, Apr, May, June, Sept, 10am-7pm daily, July, Aug. Tel. (051) 388603/389104.

DUNDALK MUSEUM AND INTERPRETATIVE CENTRE

Dundalk, County Louth

In an imaginative project, an old warehouse in central Dundalk, once belonging to the P.J. Carroll tobacco company, has been transformed into an excellent town museum and interpretative centre, one of the largest and best appointed in the east of Ireland. The ground floor houses the museum, while three upper floors have galleries for exhibitions. It is also the site of Dundalk's library. Visitors to the museum are greeted by the sight of a perfectly preserved Heinkel bubble car, made in Dundalk about 1960. Dundalk has had its share of industrial tragedies, including the closure of the Great Northern Railway works, but has managed to adapt and survive. The story of many of those industries is told here, from cigarette-making and shoemaking to brewing and newspapers. Gift shop, coffee shop.

Jocelyn Street, off Clanbrassil Street. Admission charge. Open 10.30am-5.30pm Tues-Sat, 2pm-6pm, Sun, bank holidays, all year. Tel. (042) 27056/57.

DUNGARVAN MUSEUM

Dungarvan, County Waterford

This small but representative museum is housed, along with the town library, in the restored late-17th c. market house. The museum depicts the history of Dungarvan, including the building of the adjacent King John's Castle in the mid-13th c. and the arrival of the Augustinians at Abbeyside, also in the 13th c. Many old photographs show such events at fair days in Dungarvan, while old utensils include a penny farthing bicycle. The development of the town in the early 19th c. is described in detail, but the highlight of the museum is its collection of maritime material: shipwrecks are particularly well documented, notably that of the *Moresby*, lost in Dungarvan Bay on Christmas Eve 1895.

Also worth seeing near Dungarvan is the Seanachie inn where the past has been preserved beneath its thatched roof. Old whiskey jars, mirrors, signs and packets of Van Houten's cocoa, stone floors, even an old spinning wheel help keep the old times alive.

Dungarvan museum: *500 m (550 yards) from town centre, near seaside promenade. Admission charge. Open 2pm-6pm Mon-Fri, all year. Tel. (058) 41231.*

Seanachie inn: *5 km (3 miles) S of Dungarvan, just off N25 Dungarvan-Youghal road.*

EAST CLARE HERITAGE CENTRE

Tuamgraney, County Clare

St Cronan's 10th-c. church in the centre of the village of Tuamgraney, on the W shores of Lough Derg, is probably the finest surviving example of an early Christian church in Ireland. It's also claimed to be the oldest church still used for services in either Ireland or Britain; Church of Ireland services are still held in the 12th-c. chancel. The church has a dual purpose: the 10th c. nave houses the heritage centre, which details the history of the area, including its associations with Brian Boru who enlarged the church in 1007 and restored the now vanished round tower beside it. The centre also has rare books and papers, plus a video presentation. Many artefacts from the offshore Holy

Island, which had a large and ancient religious settlement dating back to the 7th c. and earlier are planned to be moved to the centre from their present home in the National Museum. Visitors can also walk through nearby Raheen wood, one of the few primeval forests still left in Ireland.
15 km (9 miles) NW of Killaloe. Admission charge. Open 10am-6pm daily, Apr-Oct. tel. (061) 921351.

PLUNKETT EDUCATION MUSEUM

Dublin City

This small museum in the former stables of Rathmines Castle, which now houses the Church of Ireland College of Education, gives a useful insight into 19th-c. classroom life. The museum is named after William Plunkett, the Archbishop of Dublin who brought the Protestant schools into the national school system. The recreation of an old classroom is complete with desks, a peat fire and attendance book.
Upper Rathmines Road, Dublin 6. Admission free. Open by arr only. Tel. (01) 497 0033.

ENNISCORTHY MUSEUM

Enniscorthy, County Wexford

Wexford's county museum has an incredible collection packed into three floors of this late 16th-c. castle. A stone plaque at the entrance to the castle marks the first flight between Britain and Ireland, which landed near Enniscorthy on 22 April 1912. The ground floor includes a brougham carriage that once belonged to Moira O'Neill, the Glens of Antrim poetess, a late-18th c. sedan chair and a jaunting car. Upstairs rooms include an ecclesiastical collection, a section on the 1916-1923 fight for independence and, appropriately for Enniscorthy, a section on the 1798 uprising. Vinegar Hill, the last battlesite of that uprising, can be seen from the castle windows. There's also a police room with memorabilia from police forces all over the world. On the second floor are models of ships and old farming implements, plus detail on the nearby Carley's Bridge Potteries, founded in 1654.

24 km (15 miles) NW of Wexford on N11. Near town bridge. Admission charge. Open 10am-6pm Mon-Sat, 2pm-5.30pm Sun, Apr-Sept, 2pm-5.30pm Sun, Oct-Mar. Tel. (054) 35926.

ENNISKILLEN CASTLE

Enniskillen, County Fermanagh

Parts of the castle, surrounded by a wide moat, date back to the 15th c. and include several attractions. The castle keep, in the original Maguire stronghold, houses the regimental museum of the Royal Inniskilling Fusiliers, a regiment formed in the late 17th c. Weapons, uniforms and medals are included in the collection. Last, but by no means least, there are also displays on the natural history, folklife and archaeology of County Fermanagh, besides an audio-visual programme on the history of the Maguire clan and the town of Enniskillen. Gift and bookshop, café.

138 km (86 miles) SW of Belfast. Admission charge. Open 10am-5pm Tues-Fri, 2pm-5pm Mon, Sat, May-Sept, also 2pm-5pm Sun, July, Aug, bank holidays, 10am-5pm Tues-Fri, Oct-Apr. Tel. (01365) 325000.

FETHARD MUSEUM

Fethard, County Tipperary

This glorious ragbag of a collection began in an old railway station and has expanded considerably. The number of exhibits runs to thousands, and includes an extraordinary range of household items and utensils, including Victorian prams. Transport of all kinds is a strong theme. Outside, the museum has one of the best collections of old farm machinery in Ireland. Also worth seeing in Fethard are the medieval town walls, very extensive and sensitively restored.

Fethard is 14 km (9 miles) N of Clonmel on the R689. Admission charge. Open 10.30pm-5pm daily, July, Aug, 1pm-5pm Sun, all year, or by arr. Tel. (052) 31516.

FINDLATER'S MUSEUM

Dublin City

Findlater's grocery stores were renowned in the Dublin

area from the late 19th c. to the 1960s, but were superseded by the supermarket era. Many artefacts from the old counter service stores are preserved in the museum at present-day Findlater's, a wine company located in the vaults beneath the old Harcourt Street railway station. The museum details the Findlater family's Scottish antecedents, its connections with Robert Burns the poet, and many photographs and other memorabilia from its chain of shops. The atmosphere of old style shopping is enhanced at the entrance to the company's premises, where a replica double-fronted shop façade has been recreated.
Harcourt Street, Dublin 2. Admission free. Open 9.30am-5.30pm Mon-Sat, all year. Tel. (01) 475 1699.

FLIGHT OF THE EARLS CENTRE
Rathmullan, County Donegal
In 1607, the great exodus of nobility, known as the Flight of the Earls, took place from the harbour here. Their flight into exile saw the end of the old Gaelic order in Ireland and within two years the plantation of Ulster began. The story of the earls is dramatically told in the centre at Rathmullan using models, artefacts, extracts from literature and stained glass. Wax figures of the two leading earls, Hugh O'Neill and Rory O'Donnell, stand at the entrance to the exhibition hall, which is divided into three areas. The centre is housed in a fort dating from Napoleonic times; a similar one on the opposite shore of Lough Swilly houses the **Fort Dunree** military museum. Flight of a different kind is illustrated at **Ramelton Heritage Centre,** where Francis Makemie was born in 1658; he emigrated in 1683 and founded the American Presbyterian church. The centre has a library, artefacts and displays.
Rathmullan, 26 km (16 miles) NE of Letterkenny. Admission charge. Open 10am-6pm Mon-Sat, 12noon-6.30pm Easter, May-Sept. Tel. (074) 58178/58131.
Fort Dunree: *16 km (10 miles) NW of Buncrana. Admission charge. Open 10am-6pm Tues-Sat, 12noon-6pm Sun, Easter-Sept. Tel. (074) 24613.*
Ramelton Heritage Centre: *13 km (8 miles) NE of*

Letterkenny. Admission charge. Open 9am-5pm daily, July, Aug, or by arr. Tel. (074) 51266.

FOXFORD WOOLLEN MILLS VISITOR CENTRE

Foxford, County Mayo

Over a century ago, the woollen mills were set up by the Sisters of Charity to provide employment in an area that was suffering great economic and social deprivation. The story of these mills, famous for their rugs and other woven products, is told in audio-visual form in the visitor centre, the *Foxford Experience*. The trials and tribulations of post-famine Mayo form a dramatic introduction to the tour of the mills, during which visitors can see Foxford rugs and tweeds being made. Exhibition centre, shop, restaurant.

24 km (15 miles) NE of Castlebar. Admission charge. Open 10am-6pm Mon-Sat, all year, 12noon-6pm Sun, May-Oct, 2pm-6pm Sun, Nov-Apr. Tel. (094) 56756.

FOYLE VALLEY RAILWAY CENTRE

Derry City

This comprehensive railway museum tells the story of the narrow gauge railways in north-west Ireland, with the exhibits housed in a purpose-built centre

Foyle Valley Railway

reminiscent of a Victorian station. Among them are samples of rolling stock from the former County

Donegal railway and the Londonderry and Lough Swilly Railway Company, as well as some steam locomotives from the County Donegal Railway. Many railway artefacts are included and some can be operated by visitors. The upper floor has more memorabilia, an electronic railway map, railway models and an audio-visual presentation.
Entrance beside city end of Craigavon Bridge. Admission charge. Open 10am-5pm Tues-Sat, all year. Tel. (01504) 265234. Railway trips, weekends only, May-Sept.

FOYNES FLYING BOAT MUSEUM
Foynes, County Limerick
A unique era in aviation history is recalled in this fascinating museum. In the late 1930s flying boats started using Foynes on the Shannon estuary as their Irish base for the trans-Atlantic crossing and during World War II Foynes became an even more important transport link. After the war, Shannon airport opened for use by piston-engined, then jet aircraft, but the glamorous days of flying boats are well recounted in this museum. Displays include the original terminal building and the radio and weather room with its original equipment. For many visitors, the highlight will be the small 1940s-style cinema which shows World War II newsreels. The centre also details the origins of Irish coffee, invented here in 1942 by the chef, Joe Sheridan, to warm up some damp, cold passengers. The tearoom is decorated in the style of that period. Shop.
37 km (23 miles) W of Limerick on S shore of Shannon estuary. Admission charge. Open 10am-6pm daily, Apr-Oct. Tel. (069) 65416.

GALWAY CITY MUSEUM
This small museum, with a quayside location beside the Spanish Arch, has a mixture of folk and medieval artefacts and documentation recalling the city's development since the 12th c. The displays include a copy of the famous 1691 map of Galway, while the city's most famous district, the Claddagh, is also

recalled. Its cottages have long since been swept away in the name of modernisation, but the name lives on,

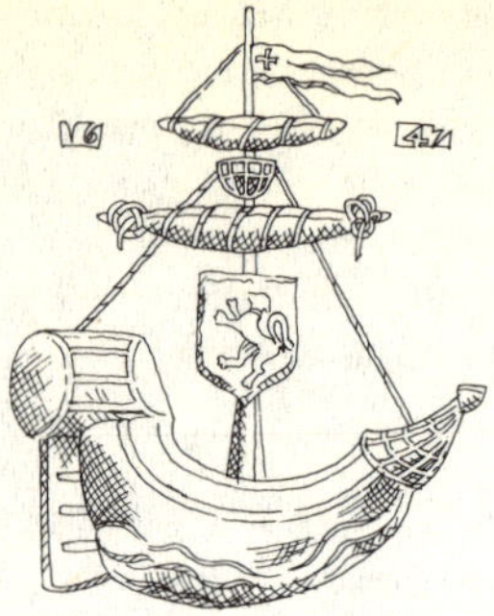

Date stone, Galway City

especially in Claddagh rings. Early photographs and other memorabilia recall the earlier days of the Claddagh, while other Galway institutions, like the Salthill tram, are also recorded.
City quaysides near Spanish Arch. Admission charge. Open 10am-1pm, 2pm-5pm daily, June-Aug. Tel. (091) 67641.

GARVAGH MUSEUM

Garvagh, County Derry

This museum and heritage centre is set in the walled garden of Garvagh House, the ancestral home of the Canning family for almost 300 years. George Canning became British prime minister in 1827. The museum, which claims to be the largest school-based museum in these islands, has artefacts covering most aspects of rural and domestic life in the 19th and early 20th c.
20 km (12 miles) S of Coleraine. Admission charge. Open 2pm-5pm Thurs, Sat, June-Aug, or by arr. Tel. (012665) 58216/58188.

GIANT'S CAUSEWAY CENTRE

Giant's Causeway, County Antrim

The Giant's Causeway itself is Ireland's most extraordinary natural location. Its 40,000 columns of rock are shaped like threepenny pieces and the whole site divides into three sections, the result of the action of the waves over the centuries. The audio-visual presentation is complemented by the interactive Causeway Exhibition, which tells the story of the area's flora and fauna and the history of tourism in this part of Ireland. Local industrial and commercial activities, such as mining and kelping, are detailed, as is the history of the Ould Lammas Fair, held every August in nearby Ballycastle. Craft shop, restaurant.

Giant's Causeway

The nearby **Causeway School museum** is housed in a former school that functioned as such from 1915 to 1962. The building was designed by Clough Williams-Ellis, who also designed houses in Cushendun in the Glens of Antrim and Portmeirion in North Wales.
22 km (14 miles) NE of Coleraine.
Giant's Causeway Centre: *Admission charge. Open 10am-7pm daily, July, Aug, 10am-4.30pm Sept-June. Tel. (012657) 31855.*
School museum: *Admission charge. Open 11am-4.30pm daily, July, Aug.*

GLENCOLUMBKILLE FOLK MUSEUM

Glencolumbkille, County Donegal

The brainchild of the late Fr James McDyer, parish priest here for many years, the museum was set up to help preserve the area's strong cultural traditions. The heart of the museum consists of three reconstructed houses, one from 1700, another from 1850 and the third from 1900. The 19th c. house has a flagstone floor and includes tools once used by a shoemaker. The early 20th-c. house is altogether more grand and includes a parlour, complete with wooden floor, linoleum, a sofa and a gramophone. Craft shop, tearoom.

25 km (16 miles) SW of Ardara. Admission charge. Open 10am-6pm Mon-Sat, 12noon-6pm Sun, Easter Sat-Oct. 6.30pm closing daily, from June 1 onwards. Tel (073) 30017.

GLENDALOUGH VISITOR CENTRE

Glendalough, County Wicklow

This low key, unobtrusive centre is a useful introduction to the whole Glendalough site, one of Ireland's most notable monastic locations, set in a new national park that will eventually extend to 30,000 ha (12,141 acres). The centre has an audio-visual presentation, *Ireland of the Monasteries*, an introduction not only to Glendalough but to the arrival of Christianity in Ireland and the spread of the Irish religious influence to Britain and mainland Europe. The centrepiece is a large model of the site as it probably looked about 1080. Outside, the well-preserved ruins include a cathedral, St Kevin's church and a round tower, 33 metres (100 ft) high and one of the best preserved in Ireland.

51 km (32 miles) SW of Dublin. Turn off the Dublin-Wexford N11 at Kilmacanogue and take the R755. Admission charge. Open 9.30am-5pm daily, mid-Oct-mid-Mar, 9.30am-6pm mid-Mar-May, Sept-mid-Oct, 9am-6.30pm daily, June, July, Aug. Tel. (0404) 45325.

GUINNESS VISITOR CENTRE

Dublin City

Guinness and Dublin are synonymous; the dark brew

has been produced on this site since 1759. The Hop Store is an ingeniously converted warehouse that contains an impressive multimedia presentation on the history of Guinness, which highlights its contribution to Irish social and literary life. This presentation is complemented by the brewing gallery that depicts the traditional and contemporary methods of making Guinness. Although there's a lot of old equipment and a fair amount of technical information, it all slips down as easily as the familiar pint. On the ground floor, visitors can enjoy a free sample. The building is also used for visiting exhibitions. Gift shop.
Crane Street, off Thomas Street, Dublin 8 (signposted). Admission charge. Open 10am-3pm, Mon-Fri, all year. Tel. (01) 453 6700.

HARBOUR MUSEUM
Derry City
The former offices of the Derry Harbour Commissioners, built around 1880, have been turned into a splendid maritime museum. The museum recalls the heady days of Derry shipbuilding, which flourished in the 19th century, and in World War II. Then, ships of the countries in the Allied war effort tied up in Derry and their crews brought an exotic foreign influence to the city. The museum is awash with models, maps, drawings and photographs.
Derry city centre, beside Guildhall. Admission free. Open 9am-1pm, 2pm-5pm Mon-Fri, all year. Tel. (01504) 365151.

HILL OF TARA, COUNTY MEATH
The Hill of Tara, with its splendid views stretching far across the Midlands, was once the seat of the High Kings of Ireland, the main centre of political and religious power in pre-Christian Ireland. The hilltop with its closely-cropped grass has little to show these days, apart from the mounds. The layout of the site is well signposted. The early 19th-c. Church of Ireland church at the approach to the site has been turned into a visitor centre; the highlight is an audio-visual presentation, *Tara, Meeting Place of*

Heroes. Nearby tea rooms, craft and book shop.
10 km (6 miles) SE of Navan. Take the signposted turn off the Navan-Dublin N3. Admission charge to visitor centre. Open 9.30am-5pm daily, May-mid-June, mid-Sept-end Oct, 9.30am-6.30pm, daily, mid-June-mid-Sept. Tel. (046) 25903.

HISTORIC SCIENCE CENTRE

Birr Castle, County Offaly

This ambitious project plans to tell the story of Ireland's scientific heritage, focusing not just on the remarkable work of the Rosse family from Birr, but on Ireland's many other scientific pioneers. The first phase, due to open in 1996, is the restoration of the huge telescope devised by the third Earl of Rosse in the early 1840s and, for 70 years, the largest astronomical telescope in the world. Other aspects of the new centre will feature the device made by the fourth Earl of Rosse for measuring the heat of the moon, Victorian photography (a great interest of the third Earl's wife), microscopy (another family interest) and details of the world's first steam turbine ship, also the handiwork of a family member. The new centre will complement the recently opened heritage centre in the town.
Entrance through castle gateway, 0.8 km (0.5 miles) W of Birr town centre. Admission charge. Domain open daily, all year, as will be the scientific centre. Tel. (0509) 20056.
Heritage Centre: *John's Hall. Admission charge. Open 2.30pm-5.30pm daily, Apr-Sept. Tel. (0509) 21450.*

HOWTH TRANSPORT MUSEUM

Howth, County Dublin

This museum, in the grounds of Howth Castle, has fine examples of old vehicles crammed into every corner: public transport, commercial and public utilities and military transport. Most striking exhibit is the fully-restored double-deck tram, Number 9, from the Hill of Howth tramway, which ran from 1902 until 1959. Alongside it, but less glamorous, is a standard Dublin double-deck tram which was in service from 1928 until the Dublin tramway system closed down in 1949. One of the world's oldest electric tramway cars is being restored; it dates from about 1883 and was used on the Portrush and Giant's Causeway tramway, which also closed in 1949. A double-deck green-painted Dublin bus, once part of a familiar fleet in the city through the 1950s and 1960s, is complemented by two blue-and-cream-painted buses, one double deck, the other a single decker, that once belonged to the Great Northern Railway company.

On Dublin side of Howth village, 0.8 km (0.5 miles) past turn for Howth Lodge Hotel (signposted). Admission charge. Open 11am-6pm daily, May-Sept, 12noon-5pm Sat, Sun, bank holidays, Oct-Mar. Tel. (01) 848 0831/847 5623.

HUNT MUSEUM

Limerick

One of Ireland's finest collections is set to move to striking new premises: the Hunt Collection, presently in the University of Limerick, is moving to the city's 18th-c. Custom House, Limerick's finest Georgian building, standing on the banks of the River Shannon. In its new setting, the museum will use modern video and multi-media techniques in its main galleries, while it will also have a visible storage gallery. The museum is truly international in its collection, and includes works by Gauguin and Picasso and a bronze by Leonardo da Vinci, even a Greek silver coin considered to be one of the Biblical 30 pieces of silver. There is also Irish archaeological material, including Neolithic flints, Bronze Age gold, the 8th-c. Antrim Cross and penal crucifixes from the 18th and 19th c. These medieval treasures are the finest in Ireland outside the National Museum in Dublin.

Old Custom House, near St Mary's cathedral. Admission charge. Open 10am-5pm Mon-Sat, all year. Tel. (061) 333644.

INIS OÍRR HERITAGE HOUSE

Aran Islands

Innis Oírr (Inisheer) is the smallest of the three Aran Islands and the Ceárd Shiopa Inis Oírr on the island promotes Aran culture and art. Next door is the heritage house, built as a traditional Aran Islands house with sturdy stone walls and a thatched roof tied down against the wind. The folk collection inside the museum details the history of island life up to the present and includes old photographs. *See also* Aran Islands.

Craft shop and museum are beside the main pier. Admission free. Open 10am-6pm daily, Apr-Sept, or by arr. Tel. (099) 75021.

INNISKEEN, COUNTY MONAGHAN

The birthplace of poet Patrick Kavanagh, in 1906, this small, attractive village has several places of interest, primarily the **folk museum** and the **Patrick Kavanagh Rural and Literary Resource Centre.** The museum, housed in a former church, has about a dozen sections. Themes covered include the old Great Northern Railway, poitín-making, schooldays, carpentry, shoemaking and blacksmithing, all redolent of rural life in the early years of this century, when the poet was growing up here. The museum also has Kavanagh's death mask. The Kavanagh centre is also in a converted church which he attended as a young boy. The centre also has a library and tours of the area are organised. Kavanagh himself is buried in the adjacent graveyard.

14 km (9 miles) W of Dundalk.

Folk Museum: *Admission charge. Open 2pm-6pm, Sun, Apr-Sept, or by arr. Tel. (042) 78109.*

Kavanagh Centre: *Admission charge. Open 11am-5pm Mon-Fri, 2pm-7pm Sat, Sun, bank holidays, all year. Tel. (042) 78560.*

IRISH AGRICULTURAL MUSEUM

near Wexford town, County Wexford

This museum, set in the grounds of Johnston Castle, displays and details the old rural way of life. In the transport section, old carts, pony traps and tractors are on view, while many of the old rural crafts are brought to life in displays that include harness-making, basket-making, a carpenter's workshop and a blacksmith's.

Farmhouse interiors are recalled in detail and the museum has a good collection of Irish country furniture. Coffee shop open July, Aug.
8 km (5 miles) SW of Wexford town, off N25 to Rosslare (signposted). Admission charge. 9am-5pm Mon-Fri, 2pm-5pm Sat, Sun, June-Aug, 9am-12.30pm, 1.30pm-5pm Mon-Fri, 2pm-5pm Sat, Sun, Apr, May, Sept-Nov, 9am-12.30pm, 1.30pm-5pm Mon-Fri, Dec-Mar. Tel. (053) 42888.

IRISH HORSE MUSEUM

Kildare, County Kildare

This museum, part of the National Stud and the Japanese Gardens adjacent to Kildare town, tells the story of the animal that has achieved mythological status in Ireland. The museum is compact but tells the history of the horse from prehistoric times to the present in a logical and appealing manner. Many medieval relics include bronze rowel spurs from the 15th c., Anglo-Norman horseshoe nails, a 12th-c. iron horseshoe, horse bones (12th c. or earlier) from Wood Quay in Dublin and a 13th c. horse skull found near Christ Church cathedral in the city. Bianconi and his mail coaches are on display; the latter was the first mode of public transport in Ireland. At its peak the service had 100 vehicles and 1,400 horses. Amid all the horse memorabilia, one exhibit stands out, that of the skeleton of Arkle, arguably the greatest ever racehorse, born in 1957. It ran its last race in 1966. Craft and gift shop, restaurant.
In the town centre, turn left (signposted) and follow the road for 1.6 km (1 mile) to the entrance to the Japanese Gardens. Admission charge. Open 9.30am-6pm daily, Feb-Nov. Tel. (045) 521251.

IRISH NATIONAL HERITAGE PARK

Ferrycarrig, County Wexford

This open-air museum has 14 separate sites in a magnificent rural setting beside the Slaney estuary, complete with winding paths, streams, ponds and an abundance of wildlife. The full-scale reconstructions

of homesteads and places of ritual and worship are archaeologically authentic. The tour begins with the Stone Age (7000 BC – 2000 BC) and includes a Neolithic farmstead. The Bronze Age reconstruction (2000 BC – 500 BC) includes a stone circle, while the Celtic/early Christian era (500 BC – AD 1169) includes examples of Ogham, the earliest Irish form of writing. The displays end with the early Norman period, 1169-1190, when the Anglo-Norman invaders arrived in Ireland: the site includes an almost Moorish-looking reconstruction of an early Norman castle.
5 km (3 miles) W of Wexford, off main N11 Dublin-Wexford road. Admission charge. Open 10am-7pm daily, Mar 17-Oct 31. Tel. (053) 41733.

IRISH WHISKEY CORNER
Dublin City
Whiskey has been distilled in Ireland for over 1,000 years, using a process originally invented in the Middle East for distilling perfume. The story of whiskey and its making is told in the Irish Whiskey Corner, in part of the old Bow Street distillery complex founded in

Making Irish whiskey

1780. All kinds of artefacts are there, calico bags for barley samples, clogs worn by the workers, the tools used for making the wooden casks, even a list of nick-names of Dublin whiskey workers. Visitors can taste different Irish whiskies made by the company in the Ball o' Malt bar. Shop.

Bow Street, off Church Street, Dublin 7. Admission charge. Tours: 3.30pm Mon-Fri, all year, also 11am Mon-Fri, summer. Tel. (01) 872 5566.

JAMESON WHISKEY HERITAGE CENTRE

Midleton, County Cork

The old whiskey distillery here has been marvellously restored. Whiskey distillation began here in 1825 and continued for 150 years before being moved to the modern distillery nearby. The world's largest pot still and many other facets of the old distillery can still be seen. Visitors can tour the complex of old buildings and inspect the maltings, corn stores, stillhouses and warehouses. The story of whiskey is graphically told, with audio-visual presentations, demonstrations, display cabinets, artefacts and working models. Shop, coffee shop.

25 km (15 miles) E of Cork on N25. Admission charge. Open 10am-6pm daily, Apr-Oct. Last tour starts 4.30pm. Or by arr. Tel. (021) 613594/613596.

JAMES JOYCE TOWER

Sandycove, County Dublin

The James Joyce industry is flourishing in Dublin as never before. Following the Joycean trail through Dublin can provide an interesting if arduous itinerary, but one essential is the Joyce Tower at Sandycove, County Dublin. Once a Martello tower, built in the early 19th c. against the threat of a Napoleonic invasion, Joyce lived here briefly in 1904 and described it in the first chapter of *Ulysses*. Thanks to Sylvia Beach the first publisher of the book, the tower was reopened as a museum in 1962. In a recent refurbishment the upstairs room has been reconstructed to look exactly as it did in *Ulysses*. The new **James Joyce Cultural Centre** in Dublin city centre, in a restored 18th c. town house, also has material on Joyce, plus an ongoing cultural programme on his work. *See also* **Nora Barnacle's House.**

Joyce Tower, Sandycove, County Dublin: *3 km (2 miles) S of Dun Laoghaire. Admission charge. Open 10am-1pm, 2pm-5pm Mon-Sat, 2pm-6pm Sun, bank holidays, Apr-Oct, or by arr. Tel. (01) 872 2077.*

Joyce Cultural Centre: *35 North Great George's Street, Dublin 1. Admission charge. Open 9.30am-5pm Mon-Sat, 12.30pm-5pm Sun, all year. Tel. (01) 873 1984/878 8547.*

KENMARE HERITAGE CENTRE

Kenmare, County Kerry

This new centre details many facets of local history, including the establishment of the town and its mine by Sir William Petty, founder of the Lansdowne estate, in 1670. The centre also uses modern audio-visual and display techniques to detail the effect of the famine in the late 1840s on the town and the lace once made by the local nuns. A separate lace display is upstairs.

Market Square. Admission charge. Open 10am-6pm Mon-Sat, Apr-Sept, also 11am-5pm Sun, July, Aug. Closed for lunch. Tel. (064) 41233.

ST KILIAN'S HERITAGE CENTRE

Mullagh, County Cavan

St Kilian, one of the great band of early Christians from Ireland who helped convert Europe to Christianity, was born in the village of Mullagh in AD 640. After evangelising the people of Franconia, he was martyred there along with his two Irish companions in AD 689. Using maps, photographs, statuettes, manuscript facsimiles and art reproductions, the centre tells the story of St Kilian and this early period of church history. An audio-visual presentation on the saint's life and the Mullagh/Würzburg connection can be seen. Craft shop, coffee shop.

10 km (6 miles) SE of Virginia. Admission charge. Open 10am-6pm Mon-Sat, 12noon-6pm Sun, Easter-Oct. Tel. (046) 42433.

KILKENNY, COUNTY KILKENNY

Ireland's most perfect medieval town is packed with fascinating sites. Best place to start is **Kilkenny Castle,** opposite the Kilkenny Design Centre. The castle was built over eight centuries ago and restoration is almost completed. For 550 years, the Anglo-Norman Butler family lived here and their way of life

Fireplace detail, Kilkenny Castle

in medieval times is recreated, together with life in the 19th c. when the castle became a Victorian country house. The drawing room is preserved as it was, as is the Long Gallery with its fine Carrara marble fireplace. Outside, the park has also been restored. Audio-visual presentation. Tea room.

In Kilkenny's main Parliament Street, **Rothe House,** built between 1594 and 1610, is now a museum. The collection includes furniture, pictures, costumes, and many local curiosities, including old musical instruments and details of the first ever Irish aeronautical patent, taken out in 1856.

St Canice's Cathedral (C of I), at the foot of the Main Street, is one of Ireland's finest churches. Its library has about 3,000 books printed in the 16th and 17th c., while the top of the round tower, beside the cathedral, is the best vantage point for an overview of this historic city.

Kilkenny Castle: Admission charge. Open 10.30am-5pm

daily, Apr, May, 10am-7pm daily, June-Sept, 10.30am-5pm Tues-Sat, 11am-12.45pm, 2pm-5pm Sun, Oct-Mar. Tel. (056) 21450.
Rothe House: *Admission charge. Open 10.30am-5pm Mon-Sat, 3pm-5pm Sun, Apr-Oct, 3pm-5pm Sat, Sun, Oct-Mar. Tel. (056) 22893.*
St Canice's Cathedral: *Open daily, all year.*

KILLALOE HERITAGE CENTRE

Killaloe, County Clare

Killaloe, that historic town at the S end of Lough Derg, has a fine new heritage centre at the town end of the historic 13-arch bridge across the river Shannon. The centre also doubles as the town's tourist information office. The flora and fauna of the district are highlighted, together with details of old waterways craft. An old Shannon barge has been replicated, with its captain's cabin, and is accompanied by a video presentation on these old boats.
21 km (14 miles) NE of Limerick. Admission charge. Open 10am-6pm daily, Apr-Sept. Tel. (061) 376866.

KILMAINHAM GAOL

Dublin City

Doorway, Kilmainham gaol

This grim building has been restored, although the cells have been left as they were; a new exhibition building has now been added to help tell the story of Ireland's struggle for independence between the 1780s and the early 1920s. The school once run by the Pearse brothers at Rathfarnham has now been turned into a museum; the life and times of Patrick Pearse, leader of the 1916 Rising, and his brother, Willie, are described through photographs, manuscripts and mementoes, plus an audio-visual presentation. Tearooms.

***Kilmainham Gaol:** Near Royal Hospital. Admission charge. Open 10am-6pm daily, May-Sept, 1pm-4pm Mon-Fri, 1pm-6pm, Sun, Oct-Apr. Tel. (01) 453 5984.*

***Pearse museum:** Grange Road, Rathfarnham, Dublin 16. 10 km (6 miles) S of city centre. Admission charge. Open 10am-1pm, 2pm-4pm daily, Nov-Jan, 10am-1pm, 2pm-5pm daily, Feb-Apr, Sept, Oct, 10am-1pm, 2pm-5.30pm daily, May-Aug. Tel. (01) 493 4208.*

KILMORE QUAY MARITIME MUSEUM

Kilmore Quay, County Wexford

The *Guillemot II*, an old lightship, stands guard at the top of the harbour in Kilmore Quay, while work goes on all around her, turning the harbour into one of Ireland's main fishing ports and creating a marina. The ship was built in Leith, near Edinburgh, in Scotland after World War I, with German reparations, to replace an earlier vessel sunk during that war. The interior of the ship gives an excellent idea of shipboard life in the old days, complete with captain's cabin, crew's quarters and cramped kitchen.

More than that, it has been packed with maritime artefacts, everything from a 200 year old compass and binnacle to a whale's backbone. The history of the Irish Navy from 1922 onwards is detailed and so too is the story of Irish Shipping, until it was scuppered in 1982. About 1,000 shipwrecks lie off the south-east coast and many of them are detailed here, while another section is full of figureheads. This fascinating shipborne museum is complemented by the maritime artefacts in James Kehoe's pub on Kilmore Quay's main street of thatched cottages. The lounge bar of the Hotel

Rosslare, on the cliffs above Rosslare Harbour, 25 km (15 miles) NE also has interesting sea items.
25 km (15 miles) SW of Wexford. Admission charge, also charge for boats to nearby Saltee islands. Open 12noon-6pm daily, June-Sept, or by arr. Tel. (053) 29655.

KILRUSH, COUNTY CLARE

This small harbour town on the N shores of the Shannon estuary boasts two heritage centres. Scattery Island, just offshore, has ruins of religious buildings; its monastery was founded in the 6th c. and the well-preserved round tower is unique in Ireland in having its entrance at ground floor level. The **Scattery Island Centre,** devoted to the island, its monasticism and wild-life, is in Kilrush town. Also in the town, the old town hall has been converted into a **heritage centre** showing the development of Kilrush from the end of the 18th c., as a planned town owned by the Vandaleur family.
Scattery Island Centre: *Merchant's Quay. Admission charge. Open 9.30am-6.30pm daily, June-Sept. Tel. (065) 52139/52144.*
Heritage centre: *Town centre. Admission charge. Open 10am-5.30pm daily, Mon-Sat, 12noon-4pm Sun, May-Sept. Tel. (065) 51047.*

KILTIMAGH, COUNTY MAYO

The old railway station has been turned into a museum, with many domestic and farm utensils and artefacts dating from the late 19th and early 20th c. It features people with local connections who made good at home or abroad, including Gene Tunney, the world heavyweight boxing champion and Mike Hogarty who supervised the first US Apollo moon landing.
25 km (15 miles) E of Castlebar. Admission charge. Open 12noon-6pm Mon-Fri, 2pm-6pm Sat, Sun, June-Sept. Tel. (094) 81494.

KING JOHN'S CASTLE

Limerick

This majestic 13th-c. edifice, on the banks of the River

Shannon, lies at the heart of medieval Limerick. Pre-Norman Limerick has been excavated and is well presented to the visitor, while the castle itself, with gate house, battlements and towers, has been restored. Models, three dimensional displays and graphics are used to tell the story of medieval history, not only within the city itself, but in Ireland as a whole. A highlight is the multimedia presentation, the *Story of Limerick*, which gives a graphically detailed account of the city's turbulent past. Directly across the river by nearby Thomond Bridge is the stone where the 1691 Treaty of Limerick was said to have been signed. *See also:* **Limerick Museum.**

Castle Street, near Thomond Bridge. Admission charge. Open 9.30am-5.30pm daily, Apr-Oct, 12noon-5.30pm Sun, Nov-Mar. Tel. (061) 411201.

KINSALE MUSEUM

Kinsale, County Cork

This museum, on the first floor of the 17th-c. former town hall, is packed with memorabilia relating to the town, everything from royal charters to the *Lusitania* disaster. Town crafts, including silvermaking and lace-making, are displayed while the museum also has details on the black cloaks worn by the women of the town until recently.

Also worth seeing in Kinsale are the 16th c. Desmond Castle in the town centre and St Multose church. Charles Fort, begun in the late 17th c., stands overlooking Kinsale harbour. Two more centres are planned for Kinsale, a town heritage centre, scheduled to be built in the old mill opposite St Multose church, and a wine museum. The latter will celebrate the Wine Geese, the Irish wine experts and owners who contributed to the wine industries in locations such as Bordeaux in France, Jerez in Spain, Chile and California; it's planned to be located in the Desmond Castle.

Kinsale museum: *Admission charge. Open 11am-5pm Mon-Sat, 3pm-5pm Sun, all year. Tel. (021) 772044.*

Charles Fort: *5 km (3 miles) S of Kinsale. Admission charge. Open daily, Apr-Sept. Tel. (021) 772263.*

Wine Museum: Details, Peter Barry. Tel. (021) 774026.

KNOCK FOLK MUSEUM

Knock, County Mayo

The museum details the Apparition of the Virgin Mary at Knock in 1879, which has been drawing pilgrims here ever since; other sections depict facets of life in rural Ireland: the thatched cottage, traditional furniture and former modes of transport; another section details items from Gaelic Athletic Association history, while the old-style schoolroom, with wooden desks, inkwells and inspectors' reports from 1865 to 1901, recalls the old teaching era. Fittingly, this detailed view of old times in the West of Ireland concludes with much material on the late Monsignor James Horan, former parish priest of Knock, who did so much to develop this part of the West.

Admission charge. Open 10am-6pm daily, May-Oct, until 7pm daily July, Aug, or by arr. Tel. (094) 88100, extn 111.

LÁR NA PÁIRCE

Thurles, County Tipperary

This fast-moving presentation details the history and development of Gaelic games. Hurling has been played in Ireland for over 2,000 years and Gaelic football since the 17th c. The Gaelic Games Association (GAA) was formed in nearby Hayes Hotel in 1884. The Sam Melbourne collection, formed over many years by a native of Horse & Jockey in County Tipperary forms the basis of Lár na Páirce. Among the items featured is the world's oldest hurley. Certain themes are detailed, including Protestant connections with the GAA. The first President of Ireland, Douglas Hyde, a Protestant, supported the GAA, while its current president (until 1997), Jack Boothman, is of similar persuasion. Sam Maguire, who donated the famous football cup, was also a Protestant. Broadcast coverage of Gaelic games includes videos of historic games and radio commentaries in Irish and English including, inevitably, the most famous GAA commentator of all, Micheál Ó Hehir.

Slievenamon Road, off Liberty Square. Admission charge. Open 10am-6pm daily, Mar-Oct. Tel. (0504) 23579.

LARNE, COUNTY ANTRIM

The port town of Larne has two heritage locations, the **Larne and District Historical Centre** and **Larne Borough Council interpretative centre.** The Historical Centre has a recreated traditional kitchen and blacksmith's forge, together with many old artefacts, family memorabilia and photographs, all creating a sense of Larne in the past. Space is limited and it is planned to move to larger premises shortly. The interpretative centre was opened in 1992 and besides housing a tourist information office, has a three-dimensional presentation on the history of the Coast Road.

***Larne and District Historical Centre:** Carnegie Arts Centre, Victoria Road, Larne. Admission free. Open 2pm-5pm Tues-Sat, May-Oct, 2pm-5pm Tues-Fri, Nov-Apr. Tel. (01574) 279482.*

***Larne Borough Council interpretative centre:** Narrow Gauge Road, Larne. Admission free. Open 10am-4pm Mon-Sat, all year, 9am-7.30pm Mon-Fri, 9am-6pm Sat, July, Aug. Tel. (01574) 260088.*

FRANCIS LEDWIDGE COTTAGE

Slane, County Meath

Francis Ledwidge, the poet, was born in Slane in 1887 and was killed in action at Ypres on 31 July 1917. The family home, built the year before Ledwidge, one of nine children, was born, has been carefully preserved. The neat cottage has material on the poet; copies of his correspondence include letters to and from his mentor, Lord Dunsany. A newspaper cutting shows his lordship proclaiming the discovery of a new Irish poet (Ledwidge) then aged 22. Seven years later he was killed by a shell on the Western Front and a shell fragment from Ypres is in the display. At the back of the house is a peaceful hillside garden.

Slane, County Meath. At crossroads in Slane, take the N51 Drogheda road for 0.8 km (0.5 mile). Admission charge.

Open 9am-1pm, 2pm-7pm daily, all year. Tel. (041) 24285/24244.

LIFEFORCE MILL

Cavan, County Cavan

This mill, which dates from the early 1840s (milling in Cavan goes back to the 16th c.), has been well restored to its original state. The restoration includes the mill machinery, waterwheel and turbine included; the water-driven turbine is a rare McAdam model, manufactured in the 1850s. Tearoom.

The Mill Rock, Bridge Street, off Main Street. Admission charge. Open 10am-6pm Tues-Sun, all year. Tours four times daily, at 11am, 12noon, 3pm and 4pm. Tel. (049) 62722.

LIFFORD HERITAGE CENTRE

Lifford, County Donegal

Just across the River Foyle from Strabane, Lifford was and is a stronghold of the O'Donnell clan, a fact reflected in this new centre. Located in the old courthouse (built 1746) it has several themes. Upstairs, a storyboard area depicts the history of Lifford until the present century, with historic items in display cases. This history is amplified by a short audio-visual presentation in the Manus O'Donnell Room. A further display area tells the story of Lifford during the Plantation. The courtroom scene recreates famous trials held here. Finally, the centre houses many geneaological records on the O'Donnells and other Donegal clans.

24 km (15 miles) SW of Derry. Admission charge. Open 10am-6pm Mon-Sat, 2pm-6pm Sun, Easter-Oct. Tel. (074) 41733.

LIMERICK MUSEUM

Limerick

Occupying two 18th-c. houses in the restored John's Square, the museum chronicles the city's history since 5000 BC. The museum is excellent, not only on the area's prehistory but on the city in the 19th and

20th c., its crafts and trades, and also the Soviet set up in Limerick after World War I. Local silverware, Limerick lace and old coinage are all part of the collection, which also has the Nail from the long-demolished Limerick Exchange built at the end of the 17th c. Traders here paid on the nail, hence the modern expression. What's left of Limerick's old city walls can be seen nearby. *See also* **King John's Castle.**
John's Square. Admission charge. Open 10am-1pm, 2.15pm-5pm Tues-Sat, all year. Tel. (061) 417826.

LINEN CENTRES
Lisburn, Banbridge and Benburb
Three separate centres tell the story of linen, once a mainstay of textile manufacturing in Northern Ireland and now enjoying a revival. The **Irish Linen Centre,** part of the excellent town museum in Lisburn, traces the development of linen-making in all its aspects from the 17th c. onwards, and highlights scutching and

Irish Linen Centre, Lisburn

weaving. The centre also has a short audio-visual presentation on the history of a fictional linen firm. A spinner's cottage and the grim Victorian mill era are recreated. The centre also has an outstanding collection of old costumes. Craft shop, restaurant.

Fergusons in Banbridge is the only maker in the world of double damask linen and its exhibition centre relates both the story of linen and of the firm itself. The **Benburb Valley Heritage Centre** is in a former linen mill and has a fine collection of linen-making machinery, including an 1899 steam engine. The centre captures well the sights and sounds of an old linen mill, with its warping, weaving, dyeing and beetling.

Irish Linen Centre: *Market Square, Lisburn, County Antrim BT28 1AG. Admission charge. Open 9.30am-5.30pm Mon-Sat (9pm Thurs), 2pm-5.30pm Sun, all year. Oct-Mar, closes at 5pm. Tel. (01846) 663377.*

Ferguson Linen Centre: *Scarva Road, Banbridge, County Down BT32 3AU. Admission charge. Open 9.30am-4.30pm Mon-Thurs, 9.30am-12noon Fri, all year. Tel. (018206) 23491.*

Benburb Valley Heritage Centre: *Benburb, County Tyrone BT71 7LZ. Admission charge. Open 10am-5pm Tues-Sat, 2pm-5pm Sun, Easter-Sept. Tel. (01861) 549752.*

LINENHALL LIBRARY

Belfast

Founded in 1788 this is Belfast's oldest library and the last surviving subscription library in Ireland. Best known for its Irish and local studies collections, it has some 200,000 books, ranging from its unrivalled holdings of early Belfast and Ulster printing to the definitive archive of the "troubles" which started in 1969. The library derives its name from its residence for most of the 19th c. in the old White Linen Hall, which stood on the site now occupied by Belfast City Hall. Coffee shop.

17 Donegall Square North, Belfast BT1 5GD, opp. City Hall. Admission free. Open 9.30am-5.30pm Mon-Fri (until 8.30pm, Thurs, except July and Aug), 9.30am-4pm Sat, all year. Closed for week 12 July. Tel. (01232) 321707.

LISMORE, COUNTY WATERFORD

Lismore, set on the banks of the River Blackwater in west Waterford, and dominated by the Duke of Devonshire's castle, is one of Ireland's most historic towns, dating back to the foundation of its monastery by St Carthach in the 7th c. The ecclesiastical history of the town is recreated in the audio-visual show, *The Lismore Experience,* in the **Lismore Heritage Centre,** once the courthouse. Also in the centre, visitors can

see the Book of Lismore, written between the 10th and 13th c., details of the town's historic buildings and material on Robert Boyle (1627-1691), who was born in the castle and became the father of modern science in Ireland. The centre has a shop.
24 km (15 miles) W of Dungarvan.
Lismore Heritage Centre: *Admission charge. Open 10am-5pm Mon-Fri, 2pm-5.30pm Sun, Apr, May, Sept, 9.30am-5.30pm Mon-Sat, 1.30pm-5.30pm Sun, June-Aug, 2pm-5.30pm Sun,Oct. Tel. (058) 54975.*

LOCKE'S DISTILLERY

Kilbeggan, County Westmeath

Locke's is one of the venerable names in Irish whiskey distilling, dating back to the mid-18th c. The first of three generations of Lockes took over in 1843, the distillery ceased production in 1954 and closed in 1957. Fortunately a new generation of Locke's whiskey has returned to the market and thanks to local community effort in Kilbeggan the old distillery has been preserved as a museum. Much of the equipment once used at the distillery is still in place, including the brewing vats, the millstones and the mash tuns. At each stage, the complicated details of the distillation process are explained. Restaurant.
Kilbeggan, 32 km (20 miles) E of Athlone on the N6. Admission charge. Open 9am-6pm daily, May-Oct, 10am-4pm daily, Nov-Mar. Closed for three days at Christmas. Tel. (0506) 32134.

LORY MEAGHER HERITAGE CENTRE

Tullaroan, County Kilkenny

Lory Meagher, described as the Prince of Hurlers, lived in this 17th c. thatched house, which has been restored to its condition in 1884, the year the GAA was founded, showing how a well-off farming family of the time lived. In one bedroom of the house, the underside of the roof can be seen, complete with sods of turf lining the thatch. Beside the house is a museum devoted to the history of Gaelic games in County Kilkenny. The third part of this centre is the farm

museum, with old machinery and demonstrations of traditional farming skills. Tearoom.
Tullaroan, 15 km (9 miles) W of Kilkenny. Admission charge. Open 2pm-5pm Sat, Sun, Mar-May, Sept-Nov, 10am-5.30pm Mon-Sat, 2pm-6pm Sun, June-Aug. Tel. (056) 69107/69202.

MALAHIDE CASTLE

County Dublin

This great castle, now in public ownership, was home to the Talbot family for nearly 700 years. The house includes the original 14th-c. tower, the 15th c. Great Hall and the reception rooms, which date from the 18th c. The rooms are hung with many portraits of Irish notables and many original furnishings are still in place. Craft and gift shop, restaurant. In a nearby building the Fry Model Railway museum has many models of old trams, steam locomotives and boats on a huge working circuit, together with details on the development of transport in Ireland over the past 150 years. Craft and gift shop.
14 km (9 miles) N of Dublin. Turn off R124 just before Malahide (signposted). Admission charge. Open 10am-5pm Mon-Fri 11am-5pm Sat, Sun, bank holidays, all year. Tel. (01) 845 2655.

MAYNOOTH COLLEGE MUSEUM

Maynooth, County Kildare

In the middle of the old campus, near the 19th c. quadrangles and chapel, the **museum** commemorates the work of Rev. Nicholas Callan, professor of natural philosophy here between 1826 and 1864. He invented many items of electrical equipment, including batteries and induction coils, which are on display. The collection also includes many religious artefacts, including penal crosses, rosary beads, pictures and medals.
25 km (15 miles) W of Dublin. Admission free. Open 2pm-4pm Tues, Thurs, 2pm-5pm Sun, summer, or by arr. Tel. (01) 628 5222.

MILLMOUNT MUSEUM

Drogheda, County Louth

Drogheda's town museum is a gem among Irish museums, with a large amount of material presented carefully and devoid of high tech gimmickry. It's in a three-storey house, part of an early 19th-c. military complex; the house itself was home to the officers' mess. Among its prize exhibits are three guild banners for weavers, carpenters and broguemakers, the only such banners left in Ireland. They are augmented by a series of trade banners, including a splendid painting of River Boyne fishermen made in 1867. The basement features a stone collection, representing every county in Ireland, every country in Europe and every continent in the world. Also in the basement is a traditional kitchen, with dresser and settle bed. Old milk cans and butter moulds are complemented by a selection of washing machines, including an 1852 rotary model. Many of the town's old industries, including its iron foundry, brewing, linen making and shoe making are featured.

The former Governor's House, across the courtyard, is used for exhibitions, while by climbing the steps to the adjacent Martello tower, visitors can enjoy an unrivalled view of the town and its surroundings. The courtyard also has a restaurant.

Off Dublin road, on Dublin side of River Boyne road bridge. Admission charge. Open 10am-6pm Tues-Sat, 2pm-6pm Sun, Apr-Oct, 2pm-5pm Wed, Sat, Sun, Nov-Mar. Tel. (041) 33097.

MIZEN HEAD SIGNAL STATION

Mizen Peninsula, County Cork

The visitor centre in the signal station at Mizen Head gives a unique insight into lighthouse workings. The island at the tip of the peninsula, on which the signal station is located, is reached by an early-20th-c. suspension bridge. The fog signal sounded out until the 1970s, while the last lighthouse keepers left the Mizen in 1993, when the lighthouse was automated. Their kitchen and bedroom have been kept as they were. An audio-visual presentation is staged in the old engine room.

25 km (15 miles) SW of Schull. Admission charge. Open 10am-6pm daily, June-Sept, or by arr. Tel. (028) 35225/35253.

MONAGHAN COUNTY MUSEUM

This award-winning museum, located in a grey stone building on a hillside, has two floors devoted to the museum exhibits and an art gallery. The museum highlights the development of the area from the time of the first settlers, between 5500 BC and 2500 BC, right up to 1990. Sections cover the movement towards Independence earlier this century. The highlight of the museum is undoubtedly the 15th-c. Cross of Clogher, an oak cross covered with bronze and semi-precious metals, depicting figures of the saints. The old Great Northern Railway, once a vital communications link, is featured in one section, complete with old station master's cap, a carriage door key and a chain and whistle, besides many old railway posters. Other sections include linen making in the town, a craft that had virtually expired here by 1850, and lace making, particularly at Carrickmacross and Clones.

Also in Monaghan is the exhibition centre in the **St Louis Convent,** the mother house of the order in Ireland. The centre tells the story of the order from the time it arrived in Ireland in 1895.

Museum: *Admission free. Open 11am-1pm, 2pm-5pm Tues-Sat, all year. Tel. (047) 82928.*

Convent: *Admission charge. Open 10am-12noon, 2pm-4pm Mon, Tues, Thurs, Fri, 2pm-4pm Sat, Sun, all year. Tel. (047) 83529.*

MORRISSEY'S PUB

Abbeyleix, County Laois

Very little has changed in this pub over the past one hundred years, yet it's a lively meeting place for local people and visitors. The old mahogany counters are still in place, together with the shelves (most Irish pubs once doubled as grocery stores). The old packets, tins and advertising posters date back to early this century. Beside the pot-bellied stove, the delivery bicycle,

complete with bell and basket, awaits the call. Abbeyleix is also due to have its own heritage centre shortly, which will highlight the town's early 20th c. carpet factory, long closed, which made carpets for the *Titanic*.
14 km (9 miles) S of Portlaoise on the N8 Dublin-Cork road. Open daily. Tel. (0502) 31233.

MUCKROSS HOUSE

Killarney, County Kerry

This Elizabethan-style mansion, built in the early 1840s, retains much of its original decor. The rooms on the ground floor, the library, dining-room and drawing-room, are all lavishly decorated, while the first floor rooms, including nursery and old-fashioned bathroom, are more homely. The windows at the rear of the house look out on the magnificent gardens sweeping down to the lake. More delights are in the basement: not only is there an old wine cellar, but an old dairy. Craft skills are practised here, including bookbinding, pottery and weaving. Outside is the most recent development, the three working farms that make up **Muckross Traditional Farms** and designed to show the lifestyles and farming traditions of County Kerry in the 1930s, before electricity. Muckross House and traditional farms are in the Killarney national park, where other sites to be seen include Muckross Abbey, founded in 1448, yew and oak woods and the only native herd of red deer in the country.
6 km (4 miles) S of Killarney town centre on N71. Admission charge to house and farms, admission free to national park and Muckross gardens.
Muckross House: *Open 9am-5.30pm daily, all year (7 pm July, Aug).*
Traditional farms: *Mar 17, Easter, 10am-7pm Sat, Sun, Apr, daily, May-Oct. Tel. (064) 31440.*

MUSEUM OF IRISH TRANSPORT

Killarney, County Kerry

This museum is a veritable cornucopia of transport memorabilia. Not only does it have many vintage and veteran cars, but also bicycles and fire engines, even the reconstruction of a vintage garage workshop, complete with tools and spare parts. The display of sparking plugs goes back to 1899. Cars on display include an 1898 Benz, brought in to Ireland by Dr J.F. Colahan of Blackrock, County Dublin. This car was the very first to take to Irish roads. Also on show is a 1904 Belgian-made Germain, a truly luxury car, but one of only four survivors of this marque. Other, more basic models on show include an Austin Seven from 1930 and an Austin 10 from 1934. The 1952 Volkswagen was one of the first Beetles to be assembled in Ireland, by the O'Flaherty group, at Shelbourne Road, Ballsbridge, Dublin. The cycle collection has about 20 machines dating from 1850 to the 1930s and include a bone shaker, made about

1898 Benz, Museum of Irish Transport

1865, and claimed as Ireland's oldest bicycle.
Scott's Gardens. Admission charge. Open 10am-6pm daily, all year. Tel. (064) 32638.

NATIONAL MUSEUM

Dublin City

The façade of the National Museum exactly mirrors that of the National Library; the two buildings are separated by the entrance to Leinster House, home of the Dáil and Seanad. On the ground floor of the museum, prehistoric artefacts include the Lurgan bogboat, dug out of a bog in County Galway early this century and the oldest surviving Irish boat, made about 2500 BC. Medieval treasures include the Ardagh hoard from County Limerick, a collection of highly-decorated croziers, including one from Lismore, County Waterford, made about 1100, and 12th c. book shrines. On the first floor, treasures include Irish silver from the 18th c. and glassware from the 19th c. Among

Ardagh chalice, National Museum

the silver pieces are a mace from Bandon, County Cork (1700) and two maces and the seal of Navan, made in Dublin in 1680. The Merrion Row entrance is to an exhibition area, while the approach to the Natural History museum is from Merrion Square West. Although the museum has been well refurbished in recent years, most of its collection is being moved to the former Collins Barracks site, near Heuston Station, which should prove an imaginative new venue. The first phase should be open in mid-1996, and new sections will include Irish furniture, silver and military memorabilia. Book and gift shop, café.
Kildare Street, Dublin 2. Admission free. Open 10am-5pm, Tues-Sat, 2pm-5pm, Sun, all year. Tel. (01) 677 7444.

NATIONAL PRINT MUSEUM
Dublin City
This new museum, due to be functional by early 1996, will recall the long and now defunct history of traditional hot metal printing. It's set in the former garrison chapel at Beggar's Bush; the barracks here were used by the British military until their withdrawal in 1922.

The ground floor of the museum has examples of old printing machinery, including hand presses, hot metal typesetting machines and proofing presses. The earliest piece of equipment is from the 18th c., one of the first examples of automation in the printing craft – a hand caster which produced a single letter of type. The mezzanine floor shows the progression of printing right up to the present day, using display cabinets of material and videos. Gift shop, coffee shop.

Also in the Beggar's Bush complex is the **Irish Labour History Society** museum, which depicts episodes from trade union history, with photographs, news clippings and other archive material.

Beggar's Bush, Haddington Road, Dublin 4. Off Northumberland Road, 0.8 km (0.5 mile) on city side of Jurys Hotel.

National Print Museum: *Admission charge. Open daily, all year. Tel. (01) 660 3770/874 6639.*

Irish Labour History Museum: *Admission free. Open 10am-4.30pm Mon-Fri, all year. Tel. (01) 668 1071.*

NEWGRANGE, COUNTY MEATH

Several places of interest are grouped on this site, led by the Newgrange passage tomb, built 5,000 years ago and regarded as the world's first solar observatory. At the winter solstice on 21 December, the rays of the

Entrance stone, Newgrange

sun shine directly down the passageway; during tours, the effect is recreated by electric light. The great mound of Knowth, nearby, dates from about 2000 BC to 2500 BC, has two passage tombs and 17 satellite tombs.

Knowth also has the greatest collection of passage tomb art ever discovered in Europe. The third site here, Dowth, remains closed for excavations. The Office of Public Works is building a Boyne Valley Interpretative Centre at Donore (due to open in 1996) on the other side of the River Boyne, which will explain in detail, using modern display and audio-visual techniques, the history and development of the whole Newgrange site. Also in this immediate area, it's worth seeing the collection of old farm machinery, the cooper's workshop and the blacksmith's forge at Óengus Lodge.
11 km (7 miles) W of Drogheda.
Newgrange: *Admission charge. Open 10am-4.30pm daily, Nov-Feb, 10am-5pm daily, Mar, Apr, Oct, 9.30am-6pm daily, May, 9.30am-7pm daily, June-Sept. Tel. (041) 24488.*
Knowth: *Admission charge. Open 10am-5pm daily, Apr-mid-June, mid-Sept, end Oct, 9.30am-6.30pm daily, mid-June-mid-Sept. Tel. (041) 24824.*
Óengus Lodge: *Admission charge. Open 10am-6pm Mon-Sat, Apr-Oct. Tel. (041) 24150.*

NEWMILLS

near Letterkenny, County Donegal

A rare venture into industrial archaeology by the Office of Public Works has seen the restoration of this milling complex, the oldest part of which is said to be between 300 and 400 years old. The mill race has been restored and so too have the two mills; one was used for flax and still has much of its old machinery, while the lower mill was used for grinding barley and oats.
3 km (2 miles) NW of Letterkenny. Admission charge. Open 11am-6.30pm daily. June-Sept. Tel. (074) 25115.

NEWRY CANAL

County Armagh

The canal was opened in 1742, linking Portadown with the sea beyond Newry; the last craft to traverse the canal did so just before World War II. Near Portadown, Moneypenny's lockhouse has been restored. Visitors can see how the lock-keepers and the lightermen lived and worked, while in the stables there's an exhibition on the local wildlife and on the history of the canal. More canal lore can be explored at the Scarva visitor centre where coal was once unloaded on the canalside dock for the local linen industry.

Moneypenny's Lock: *4 km (2.5 miles) S of Portadown. Admission free. Open 2pm-5pm Sat, Sun, Apr-Sept. Tel. (01762) 322205.*

Scarva visitor centre: *15 km (9 miles) SE of Portadown. Admission free. Open 11am-5pm Tues-Fri, 2pm-5pm, Sat, Sun, Mar-Oct. Tel. (01762) 832163.*

NEWRY MUSEUM

Newry, County Down

This small museum, located in the Arts Centre, has models of the town as it was in 1761 and in the 1930s, together with old photographs of the town. The highlight of the museum is the panelled room, decorated in the Georgian style, complete with two grandfather clocks. This room, and also an adjoining archway, were taken from an early 18th c. house in North Street in the town when the building was being demolished.

Arts Centre, Bank Parade, next to Town Hall. Admission charge. Open 11am-4pm Mon-Fri, 11am-1pm Sat, all year. Tel. (01693) 66232.

NORA BARNACLE'S HOUSE

Galway City

Nora Barnacle, wife of James Joyce, was brought up in this one-up-one-down house with no kitchen or bathroom and a tiny walled-in back-yard, near Galway city centre. Despite its lack of size, the house has some artefacts, including photographs, and great atmosphere. Stories about this remarkable couple flow freely, as if they had just visited yesterday. *See also* **James Joyce Tower.**

Bowling Green, near foot of Shop Street and St Nicholas' church. Admission charge. Open 10am-5pm Mon-Sat, May-Sept, or by arr, Sheila Gallagher. Tel. (091) 564793.

NORE VIEW FOLK MUSEUM

Bennettsbridge, County Kilkenny

This personalised museum, on the outskirts of Bennettsbridge, looking over the River Nore towards Mount Leinster and the Blackstairs mountains, has an amazing variety of items, over 10,000 in all. The man who owns it, Seamus Lawlor, has made a collection representative of modern Irish history, although it has some items dating back to 2000 BC. The penal laws, the famine, the 1916 Rising and the War of Independence all feature. Included in the displays are an old kitchen and pub, carpenter's workshop, forge and dairy, besides, most unusually, an old-style petrol station.

10 km (6 miles) SE of Kilkenny. Admission charge. Open 10am-6pm daily, all year. No telephone.

NORTH DOWN VISITORS AND HERITAGE CENTRE

Bangor, County Down

The outbuildings of Bangor Castle make an excellent setting for this historical endeavour, which is divided into several sections. In the early Christian section, the most important artefacts are the 9th c. Bangor bell and a handbell from the old monastic foundation. The centre also details the arrival of Scottish settlers in this area over 300 years ago and has an important collection of folio maps from that time. Nearer the present, Bangor's heyday as a seaside resort is recalled. Restaurant.

Rear of Bangor town hall, Castle Park Avenue. Admission free. Open 10.30am-4.30pm Tues-Sat, all year (5.30pm July, Aug), 2pm-4.30pm Sun, all year (5.30pm July, Aug). Also open bank holiday Mondays. Tel. (01247) 270371/271200.

NUMBER 29

Lower Fitzwilliam Street, Dublin City

This four-storey house, complete with basement, has been completely restored and recreated in the style of the 1790-1820 period when it was the home of a well-off wine merchant's widow. The house is owned by the Electricity Supply Board and the restoration was supervised by the National Museum of Ireland. Totally refurbished from the kitchen in the basement to the attic, the house includes servant's quarters, nursery and more formal rooms.

Number 29 Fitzwilliam Square

29 Lower Fitzwilliam Street, corner of Merrion Square and Upper Mount Street, Dublin 2. Admission charge. Open for tours, 10am-5pm Tues-Sat, 2pm-5pm Sun, all year, except for two weeks prior to Christmas. Tel. (01) 702 6165.

PEATLAND WORLD

Lullymore, County Kildare

The esoteric world of the Midlands bogs is well recaptured in this new museum, housed in restored stableyard buildings. The displays include the kitchen and hearth of an old cottage, scale models of old and new peat-fired power stations and briquette works, and presentations on the flora and fauna of the boglands. Animal, bird and insect species have been preserved. Mementoes of old turf cutting, besides implements and equipment, are shown. Many old photographs complete the display. The nearby **Lullymore Heritage Park** recreates early Christian settlements.

24 km (15 miles) N of Kildare. Take the R401 to Rathangan, then the R414. Admission charge. Open 9.30am-5pm

Mon-Fri, all year, also 2pm-6pm Sat, Sun, Apr-Oct. Tel. (045) 60133.
Lullymore Heritage Park: *Open daily, all year.*

PHOENIX PARK VISITOR CENTRE

Dublin City

The centre tells the story of the Phoenix Park, Europe's largest park, which was created as a deer park in 1662 by the Duke of Ormond. A audio-visual presentation introduces visitors to the centre, which details the many historical events that took place in the park, including the assassination of Lord Frederick Cavendish, Chief Secretary of Ireland and his deputy, Thomas Henry Burke, in May 1882. The many great meetings that have taken place here are also highlighted, including the Land League meeting of 1880, attended by 30,000. At the 1932 Eucharistic Congress, a quarter of a million men walked in procession to the Mens' Mass, while when Pope John Paul II came to the park on 29 September 1979, over a million people attended. The Papal cross can still be seen. The park still has its deer herds; the flora and fauna are well documented. Exhibition area. Nature trails.

Nearby is a restored early-17th-c. tower house, once part of the old Papal Nunciature. The recreation of the roof timbers, using oak from the park, is impressive. Tearooms.

Phoenix Park, Dublin 7. Take the main road through the park to the signposted turn for Ashtown Castle visitor centre. Admission charge. Open 9.30am-5pm daily, Mar, Oct-Nov, 9.30am-5.30pm daily, Apr, May, 9.30am-6.30pm daily, June-Sept, 9.30am-4.30pm daily, Dec-Feb. Tel. (01) 677 0095.

REGINALD'S TOWER

Waterford City

Believed to date from 1003, the circular tower is the oldest civic building in Ireland and the recently refurbished interior shows many important artefacts and documents relating to the city of Waterford, which dates back to Viking times. These include the city's

royal charters, which are most impressive. Other relics include the ceremonial swords of King Henry VIII and King John; Anglo-Norman kings used the place as a residence. The second floor of the tower, where Strongbow and Aoife were reputedly married, features a large limestone fireplace dating from the 15th c. The tower was also used as a mint, which had been established in the city in 1463.
The Quay, near Tower Hotel. Admission charge. Open 10am-5pm Mon-Sat, May-Sept. Tel. (051) 73501.

REIDY'S SHOP

Killarney, County Kerry

Although not strictly within the ambit of this guide, Reidy's traditional grocery shop is included here as it has been trading for well over a century and is one of the very few such shops in Ireland not to have succumbed to modernisation. The goods are still packed in wooden cupboards and shelves, the floor is wooden and the counter runs the length of the shop, to the bar at the back. Hooks for the Christmas turkeys and hams are still embedded in the ceiling. The shop also has one hundred varieties of sweets, sold by the quarter pound. Reidy's, which is run by the Sheehan family, even has five varieties of snuff. The shop is a marvellous and rare example of how grocery shopping used to be.
Main Street, Killarney, County Kerry. Open 9am-6pm Mon-Sat, all year. Tel.(064) 31011.

ROSCREA, COUNTY TIPPERARY

Damer House in the centre of Roscrea is a well-restored Queen Anne-style town house, dating from the 1720s, particularly noted for its staircase. Frequent exhibitions are held here. Beside the house, the garden has been replanted in the 18th-c. Georgian style, while at the front of the complex, the 13th-c. castle has been restored. Also in County Tipperary, the former jail and governor's house at **Nenagh** have been converted into a heritage centre. A traditional shop, classroom, forge and dairy have all been recreated, while the gatehouse, once occupied by condemned prisoners, has vividly recreated cells and scaffold.

Roscrea, 72 km (45 miles) NE of Limerick.

Damer House and Roscrea Castle: *Admission charge. Open 9.30am-6pm daily, June-Sept, 10am-5pm Sun, Oct-Apr. Tel. (0505) 21850.*

Nenagh, 40 km (25 miles) NE of Limerick.

Nenagh Heritage Centre: *Admission charge. Open 10am-5pm Mon-Fri, 2.30pm-5pm Sun, May-Sept, or by arr. Tel. (067) 33850.*

ROYAL GUNPOWDER MILLS

Ballincollig, County Cork

These mills were built to make gunpowder in the last decade of the 18th c. on the banks of the River Lee. After the Napoleonic wars they were closed down for 20 years before reopening and becoming a major employer in the area for the rest of the 19th c. In 1903, after the Boer War, they were finally closed. Now the mill has been reconstructed, showing just how gunpowder was made 150 years ago.

8 km (5 miles) W of Cork on N22 to Killarney. Admission charge. Open 10am-6pm daily, Easter-Sept. Tel. (021) 874430.

SKELLIG EXPERIENCE

Valentia Island, County Kerry

The centre is unique in Ireland in that it includes a boat trip. The building itself is unusual, with Valentia stone used for facing the external walls and a roof made of natural grass. The centre depicts four themes. Firstly, there's the history and archaeology of the early Christian monastery that sits atop Skellig Michael, one of the two Skellig islands off the nearby coast. Models, photographs and old artefacts, like a brass chronometer from a lighthouse, make up the exhibition, while visitors can also see an audio-visual presentation on the Skellig Michael monastery.

After touring the Skelligs centre, visitors can take to the open seas in a specially designed boat, to see the Skelligs at close quarters. The trip lasts about 1½ hours.

On Valentia Island, directly opposite the mainland village of Portmagee, where the road bridge meets the island. Admission charge. Open 10am-7pm daily, May-Oct. Tel. (066) 76306.

SLIGO COUNTY MUSEUM

Sligo Town

Located in the manse of a mid-19th-c. Congregational church, the museum has a varied selection of material from Sligo town and county, with the latter's pre-history forming an impressive centrepiece. Other material includes penal crosses, chalices, memorabilia from the War of Independence and documentation from the 19th and early 20th c. A special section is devoted to W.B. Yeats, and includes his Nobel Prize, some first editions and a complete collection of his poems, 1889-1936. In the nearby **Yeats Memorial Building,** an audio-visual presentation (summer only) shows the Yeats connections with Sligo. Yeats is buried at Drumcliff Church of Ireland church, 6 km (4 miles) N of the town.

Museum: *Stephen Street. Admission charge. Open 10.30am-4.30pm Tues-Sat, June-Sept. Tel. (071) 42212.*
Yeats Memorial Building: *Hyde Bridge. Admission charge. Open 10.30am-5pm Mon-Fri, all year. Tel. (071) 45847.*

SNEEM MUSEUM

Sneem, County Kerry

This small museum, run by Tim O'Reilly, has a wonderfully eclectic collection of local material. The museum is housed in the former courthouse, at the side of one of Sneem's two squares, and was opened in 1987. It now has around 1,500 items, from candle moulds and old furniture to school roll books and photographs of former generations of Sneem people. It has memorabilia of a former President of Ireland, the late Cearbhall Ó Dálaigh, who had strong connections with this part of south Kerry. Examination of this diverse material will be enhanced by conversation with Tim, a former wheelwright and long-time collector.

27 km (17 miles) W of Kenmare on the N70 Ring of Kerry road.
Museum: *Admission charge. Open 9am-9pm daily, June-Oct, or by arr. No telephone.*

THE SOMME CENTRE

Newtownards, County Down

This centre, opened in 1994, examines Ireland's role in World War I, especially that of the three volunteer divisions raised in Ireland, the 10th and 16th (Irish) Divisions and the 36th (Ulster) Division. Visitors are taken on a guided tour, beginning with the Home Rule crisis in 1910. An audio-visual presentation then charts the development of the war between 1914 and 1916, focussing on Gallipolli and the Battle of the Somme. A front line trench has been realistically created and visitors can also see a dramatic audio-visual recreation of the latter battle.

The War Memorial Gardens in Dublin, designed by Sir Edwin Lutyens, have been well refurbished. The gardens are dedicated to the nearly 50,000 Irish soldiers who died in World War I. All their names are listed in the Book Rooms.

Somme Heritage Centre: *4 km (2.5 miles) N of Newtownards on A21 Bangor road. Admission charge. Open 11am-6pm Mon-Sat, 12noon-6pm Sun, July, Aug, 12noon-5pm Sept-July. Tel. (01247) 823202.*
War Memorial Gardens: *Islandbridge, Dublin 8. Entrance off South Circular Road. Admission free. Open 8am-sunset Mon-Fri, 10am-sunset Sat, Sun, all year. Tel. (01) 661 3111.*

STEAM MUSEUM

Straffan, County Kildare

This museum is housed, appropriately, in a church that once stood in the Inchicore railway works in Dublin. Inside the museum, there's a fine collection of models of steam locomotives, including two used in the late 19th c. by the Great Northern Railway. The museum also has a fine selection of steam engines used for industrial propulsion, including a huge beam engine used in the Midleton whiskey distillery in County

Cork, a pumping engine employed in Jameson's distillery in Dublin, and a large beam engine installed in Smithwick's brewery, Kilkenny, in 1847. Steaming Kettle tearoom.

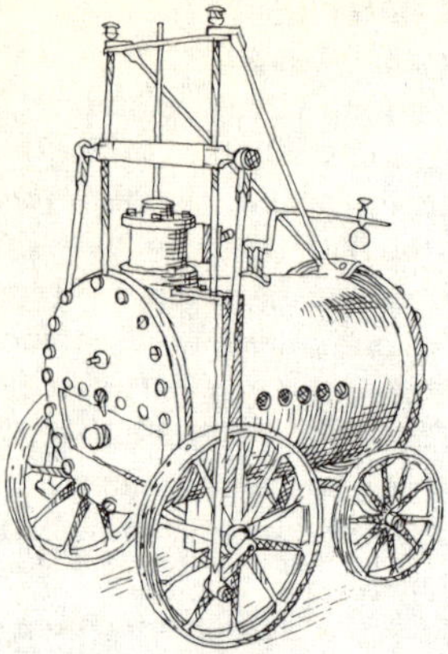

Engine at Straffan Steam Museum

32 km (20 miles) W of Dublin. Turn off N7, Dublin-Naas road at Kill. Admission charge. Open 2.30pm-5.30pm Sun, bank holidays, Apr, May, Sept, 2pm-6pm Tues-Sun, bank holidays, June-Aug, or by arr. Tel. (01) 627 3155/628 8412.

STROKESTOWN PARK HOUSE

Strokestown, County Roscommon

This remarkable house, a fine mansion built in the 1730s, was home for many years to the Pakenham-Mahon family. The last of the family to live there, Olive Pakenham-Mahon, stayed on until 1982. Thanks to the generosity of the Westward Garage group, the house and estate have been preserved. The interior of the house has been kept just as it was, so the drawing-room, dining-room, study and smoking-room, are authentically furnished. Upstairs, the bedrooms include a nursery once used by the children of the house, complete with teddy bears. The great kitchen, in a wing off the main house, has also been perfectly preserved, together with its spits and ovens; it now houses a restaurant. The outbuildings in the three stable yards have been converted into a famine museum, which tells the heartbreaking story of the famine in this area of Ireland in modern audio-visual form. There is also documentation from the period.

Strokestown Park

Also in Strokestown, at the other end of the main street, one of the widest in Europe, is **St John's Heritage Centre,** housed in a converted early 19th c. church. It has geneaological records and often stages historical exhibitions.
25 km (15 miles) W of Longford on N5.
Strokestown Park House and Famine Museum: *Admission charge. Open 11am-5pm Tues-Sun, May-Oct. Tel. (078) 30103.*
St John's Heritage Centre: *Admission charge. Open 9.30am-5.30pm Tues-Fri, 2pm-6pm Sat, Sun, May-Sept. Tel. (078) 62414.*

THEATRE ROYAL
Waterford
Waterford Corporation dates back to 1195, making it one of the oldest in northern Europe. One of the gems of City Hall is the Theatre Royal, one of only three Victorian theatres in Ireland (the others are the Gaiety in Dublin and the Grand Opera House in Belfast).

Waterford's theatre dates back to the 18th c., when it was known as the playhouse. In 1876, it was remodelled; all its Victorian features, including boxes, proscenium arch and decor have been carefully preserved.
The Mall, nearly opposite Tower Hotel. Admission free. Open 9am-5pm Mon-Fri, all year. Tel. (051) 73501.

TIPPERARY COUNTY MUSEUM

Clonmel, County Tipperary

This well-run museum has a representative selection of material on Tipperary life. Pages from 19th-c. Clonmel newspapers are accompanied by signage from the local railways and details of some of Clonmel's most famous sons, native and adopted, including Laurence Sterne, author of *Tristam Shandy*, born in the town in 1713; also Charles Bianconi, from Lombardy in Italy, founder of Ireland's first public transport system, in Clonmel in 1815.
Parnell Street. Admission free. Open 10am-1pm, 2pm-5pm Tues-Sat, all year. Tel. (052) 25399.

TOWER MUSEUM

Derry city

This award-winning museum, opened in 1992, tells the tangled story of Derry from its origins in the 6th c. right up to the present day using high technology and modern audio-visual presentation methods. Just inside the city walls, a 16th-c. tower house built originally for the local Gaelic chieftains, the O'Donnells, was reconstructed to house the museum. The many facets of the city's troubled history are impartially told and include the Siege of Derry in 1688-89, events in Ireland leading to partition in the early 1920s and the more recent troubles in Derry, including the 1969 battle of the Bogside. Derry had a civic museum from 1903 to 1951 and the Tower Museum is an admirable successor.
City centre, entrance from Linenhall Place. Admission charge. Open 10am-5pm Tues-Sat, Sept-June, 10am-5pm Mon-Sat, 2pm-5pm Sun, July, Aug. Tel. (01504) 372411.

TRALEE, COUNTY KERRY

The Ashe Memorial Hall in the centre of Tralee is home to three centres collectively known as **Kerry the Kingdom**. First, "Kerry in Colour" is an extravagant audio-visual presentation on the history of the county from prehistoric times. Kerry County Museum uses artefact, scale models and video displays to tell the story of the county from over 7,000 years ago to the present day and includes interactive videos of Kerry's Gaelic football triumphs, plus a documentary newsreel covering the period 1914-65. The third is "Geraldine Tralee", which recreates the town in the Middle Ages. Gift shop, coffee shop.

Visitors can then take the train from Tralee for the 3 km (2 miles) to Blennerville. The locomotive once ran on the old Tralee and Dingle narrow gauge railway and was returned home from a museum in Vermont. In Blennerville, the 200-year-old five storey windmill has been restored to working order. It features an audio-visual display on milling history in Ireland. There's also a display about 19th-c. emigration through Blennerville port. Gift ship, coffee shop.

***Kerry the Kingdom:** Admission charge. Open 10am-6pm Mon-Sat, (8pm in Aug), 2pm-6pm Sun, Mar-Oct. Tel. (066) 27777.*

***Blennerville windmill:** Admission charge. Open 10am-6pm Mon-Sat, 2pm-6pm Sun, Apr-Oct. Tel. (066) 21064.*

TULLYNALLY CASTLE

Castlepollard, County Westmeath

Tullynally has been the seat of the Pakenhams, the earls of Longford, since 1655. The original fortress was turned into a house in the 18th c., with the gothic façade added the following century. The evocative Victorian kitchens are well preserved, alongside the laundry, ironing and drying rooms, all packed with artefacts like the box mangle and the washing boards in the laundry. An old coach stands on display in the courtyard.

19 km (12 miles) N of Mullingar, 0.5 km (1 mile) W of Castlepollard on Granard road. Admission charge. Guided tours, daily, July, Aug, otherwise by arr. Tel. (044) 61159/61425.

TYRONE HERITAGE CENTRES

Four centres in County Tyrone each have their own not inconsiderable points of interest. In Strabane, **Gray's Printing Press** shows how the old hot metal printing worked, with examples of presses and hand-set type. The **Castlederg Visitors Centre** has a video wall, used to narrate ten stories about the social history and culture of this part of the county. Also on display is a carriage from the Castlederg tramway, which opened in 1884 and was closed after a strike in 1933. The **Newtownstewart Gateway** centre and museum includes the Dunbar collection of Victoriana, militaria, old toys, packaging and photographic equipment. The centre also has a reconstruction of a traditional farmhouse kitchen, complete with half-door. Finally, the **Sperrin Heritage Centre** tells the story of gold in the Sperrin mountains and has an audio-visual presentation. Craft shop, tearoom.

Gray's Printing Press: *Main Street, Strabane, 22 km (14 miles) SW of Derry. Admission charge. Open 2pm-5.30pm daily except Thurs, Sun, Apr-Sept. Tel. (01504) 884094.*

Castlederg centre, *20 km (12 miles) SW of Strabane. Admission charge. Open 11am-4pm Tues-Fri, 11am-5pm Sat, 1.30pm-5.30pm Sun, all year. Tel. (016626) 70795.*

Newtownstewart centre, *16 km (10 miles) SE of Strabane. Admission charge. Open 11am-4pm Mon-Fri, 11am-5pm Sat, 1.30pm-5.30pm Sun, all year. Tel. (016626) 62414.*

Sperrin centre, *Cranagh, 12 km (8 miles) E of Plumbridge. Admission charge. Open 11am-6pm Mon-Fri, 11.30am-6pm Sat, 2pm-7pm Sun, all year. Tel. (016626) 48142.*

ULSTER-AMERICAN FOLK PARK

Camphill, County Tyrone

The theme of this park is the mass emigration which took place from Ulster when, between 1700 and 1900, over two million people left to seek a new life in North America. The tour begins with the recreation of a typical Ulster village in the 18th c. One of its newest buildings was opened in 1995, a reconstruction of a Catholic Mass house from County Tyrone, dating from 1768, in the midst of penal times. The exhibition then moves on to the journey to the port, before and during the railway age, then the Atlantic passage. In the ship and dockside gallery, there's a vivid reconstruction of dockside scenes from Belfast and Derry; the buildings were moved here brick by brick.

10 km (6 miles) N of Omagh on the A5 to Newtownstewart. Admission charge. Open 11am-6.30pm Mon-Sat, 11.30am-7pm Sun, bank holidays, Easter-Sept, 10.30am-5pm Mon-Fri, Oct-Easter. Tel. (01662) 243292.

ULSTER FOLK AND TRANSPORT MUSEUM

Cultra, County Down

This extensive museum, much of it outdoors, tells the story of the North of Ireland's social and economic development, often through the recreation of old buildings and workshops. The outdoor museum covers more than 24 ha (60 acres) and includes an 1820s farmhouse from County Armagh, cottier's houses from

Cottage, Ulster Folk and Transport Museum

County Derry and County Tyrone and a mid-19th-c. farmhouse with outbuildings from near Cushendall, County Antrim. Many examples of workshops have been transposed here. Other buildings include a rectory, a church and a market/courthouse. Since all the buildings were moved from their original sites and reconstructed here, they are totally authentic. A town area is being assembled to portray, when completed, a small Ulster town with houses, shops, churches and school. The museum's farmland has many old implements and rare local breeds. There is also a strong textiles collection. Transport is well represented, with one of the highlights being the schooner *Result*, built in Carrickfergus in 1893. A road transport gallery is being developed, while perhaps the single most impressive part of the whole site is the new Irish Railway Collection. Not only have buildings been preserved, including sales kiosks from Portrush station and York Road station, Belfast, but an impressive array of carriages and locomotives from all parts of Ireland.

But of all this vast collection of railway material, by far the most extensive in Ireland, the star is undoubtedly *Maeve*, the great steam locomotive built at Inchicore railway works, Dublin, in 1939. It ran until 1958, mostly on the Dublin-Cork line and achieved a record speed of 154 kph (96 mph). Road transport and aviation are also recorded in the Dalchoolin Gallery. Frequent themed exhibitions are held. Photographic archives. Craft and book shop, restaurant, tearooms.
10 km (6 miles) NE of Belfast, off A2 Belfast-Bangor road. Admission charge. Open 10.30am-6pm Mon-Sat, 12noon-6pm Sun, July, Aug, 9.30am-5pm Mon-Fri, 10.30am-6pm Sat, 12noon-6pm Sun, Apr-June, Sept, 9.30am-4pm Mon-Fri, 12.30pm-4.30pm Sat, Sun, Oct-Mar. Tel. (01232) 428428.

ULSTER HISTORY PARK

Omagh, County Tyrone

This 14 hectare (35 acre) site, opened in 1990, tells the story of the settlement of Ireland, from the time of the first known settlers, around 8000 BC, to the Plantation period of the 17th c. Based on extensive archaeological and historical research, the park consists of full scale models of dwelling places and monuments. The Mesolithic camp reconstruction represents the earliest settlement, the huts being based on evidence from excavations at Mount Sandal, near Coleraine. Dwellings in the park range from the raths, circular-shaped houses with thatched roofs from the early Christian era, to a reconstructed Plantation settlement built after the conquest of Gaelic Irish Ulster in the early 17th c. Tearoom.

Cullion, 11 km (7 miles) NE of Omagh on B48 road to Gortin. Admission charge. Open 10.30am-6.30pm Mon-Sat, 11.30am-7pm Sun, 10.30am-7pm, bank holidays, Apr-Sept, 10.30am-5pm Mon-Fri, Oct-Mar. Tel. (016626) 48188.

ULSTER MUSEUM

Belfast

Described as the "mother museum" of Northern Ireland, it has a vast array of material; collections include fine and decorative art, archaeology and ethnography, botany, zoology and geology, local history and technology. The local history galleries illustrate political, social and industrial history in Ulster since 1600, everything from maps to coins and medals. The engineering hall has an impressive display of large steam engines and waterwheels as well as machinery once used in the linen industry. The "Made in Belfast" gallery has products made in the city over the past 100 years, from bricks and rope to bicycles and aircraft. The extensive archaeological collections have material from *c*. 7000 BC to the late 17th c., while most of the material from the Spanish Armada ships that were wrecked off the Irish coast is displayed here.

Salamander from the Girona, *Ulster Museum*

The impressive fine art collection has a wonderfully representative collection of Irish painting and sculpture from the late 17th c. to the present day.

With such a vast range of collections and material assembled since 1831, the museum merits a full day's

visit. Frequent exhibitions are held during the year. Shop, restaurant.
Botanic Gardens, Belfast BT9 5AB. Train to Botanic station, buses from City Hall, Donegall Square East. Admission free. Open 10am-5pm Mon-Fri, 1pm-5pm Sat, 2pm-5pm Sun, all year. Tel. (01232) 668251.

VINTAGE CAR AND CARRIAGE MUSEUM

Buncrana, County Donegal

This small but intriguing collection, about 25 items in all and subject to change, covers vintage and veteran cars, horse-drawn carriages and vintage motor cycles, plus model cars and railways. Among its exhibits are a 1923 vintage Rolls-Royce, a 1935 Austin Seven in immaculate condition and never restored, and a 1957 American Chevrolet.
Admission charge. Open 10am-8pm daily, June-Oct, or by arr. Tel. (077) 61130.

WATERFORD CRYSTAL VISITOR CENTRE

Waterford city

Waterford Crystal is world-renowned, one of Ireland's best regarded craft products. Glass-making started in a major way in the city in 1783 and lasted until 1851; first period Waterford is greatly treasured. It was revived after World War II. In the visitor centre, an audio-visual presentation gives the history of glass-making in Ireland from medieval times, through the establishment of the first Waterford Glass factory to present day production. Showrooms, restaurant. Near Waterford, another crystal glass company, **Tipperary Crystal**, founded by former Waterford workers, also welcomes visitors who can see the original hand-crafted methods still being used. Showrooms.
Waterford Crystal: *2.5 km (1.5 mile) W of Waterford city on the N25 Cork road. Admission charge. Open 8.30am-4pm daily, Apr-Oct, 9am-3.15pm Mon-Fri, Nov-Mar. Tel. (051) 73311.*
Tipperary Crystal: *Ballynoran, near Carrick-on-Suir, on the N24 Waterford-Clonmel road, 32 km (20 miles) NW of Waterford. Admission free. Open 9am-6pm Mon-Sat, all*

year. (Sun: showroom only 11am-6pm all year). Tel. (051) 641188.

WATERFORD HERITAGE CENTRE

Waterford city

Between 1986 and 1992 excavations in Waterford city yielded an amazing collection of artefacts, over 200,000 in all, from the Viking and medieval periods of the city's history. About 180 Viking houses were excavated and most of the objects found, dating back to between the 11th and 13th c., were perfectly preserved because of the waterlogged soil. Many examples from this wealth of material are on show in the Heritage Centre and give a clear indication of life in Viking and then medieval Waterford. The items on show include pots for the wine trade and coins. Many items of clothing, leather footwear and jewellery date from the 12th and 13th c., when Waterford port was at the peak of its trading prosperity.

Beside Reginald's Tower. Admission charge. Open 10am-1pm, 2pm-6pm Mon-Fri, 10am-1pm Sat, Apr, May, 10am-8pm Mon-Fri, 10am-1pm, 2pm-5pm Sat, June-Sept. Tel. (051) 71227.

WATERWAYS VISITOR CENTRE

Dublin city

The first artificial waterway in Ireland was dug near Lough Corrib in the 12th c. Subsequently 18th- and 19th-c. canal builders constructed waterways all over the country, including the Grand and Royal canals, linking Dublin and the Shannon, and the Ulster Canal, connecting Lough Neagh with the Erne system. Over the past 15 years interest in inland waterways has been greatly revived and the Royal Canal, closed for navigation in 1961, is now fully restored for most of its length. The three-storey Waterways centre, modernistic in its exterior and interior design, sits in the Grand Canal basin just off the River Liffey. A large relief map of Ireland shows all existing canals and also the nine canals for which restoration is planned. Other topics include canal breaches, the life of a canal family and recreations, fish and wildlife on canals. There's even a model of a Boyne coracle.

Also on a waterborne theme, the **National Maritime Museum** is located in the former Mariners' church overlooking the great harbour of Dun Laoghaire. Its exhibits include a French longboat captured during the abortive Bantry Bay invasion in 1796, the great optic, still working, from the Baily lighthouse on the other side of Dublin Bay and many models of many different types of ships and boats, plus much memorabilia. The museum has been undergoing renovations and is due to reopen in 1996.

National Waterways Centre: *off Pearse Street, Dublin 2. Admission charge. Open 9.30am-6.30pm daily, June-Sept, 12.30pm-5pm Wed-Sun, Oct-May. Tel. (01) 677 7510.*

National Maritime Museum: *Haigh Terrace, Dun Laoghaire, County Dublin, beside Royal Marine Hotel. Tel. (01) 280 0969.*

WINDMILLS

In the 18th and 19th c., the Irish countryside was dotted with windmills and their sails powered the millstones that ground the grain. Today only two restored windmills are left in Northern Ireland. The white painted **Ballycopeland Windmill**, complete with majestic sails, is the only survivor of the many windmills that once stood on the Ards peninsula, an ideal site. Built in the 1780s, this windmill was in operation until 1915. The **Knockloughrim Windmill** in County Derry was built a century later, in the 1880s, but only worked for two years before the sails were blown off. Inside the mill display panels and audio-visual presentations detail the history of Knockloughrim village, the windmill itself and wind power generation. Tearoom.

Two restored windmills can be seen in the Republic, the tall, white painted structure at **Blennerville**, County Kerry and the more homely, thatched-roof windmill at **Tacumshane**, County Wexford. This small windmill, dominated by its large sails, was built in 1846 and was restored in the 1950s.

Ballycopeland Windmill: *1.6 km (1 mile) W of Millisle. Admission charge. Open 10am-7pm Tues-Sun, Apr-Sept,*

10am-4pm Sat, Sun, Oct-Mar. Tel. (01247) 861413.

***Knockloughrim Windmill:** 5 km (3 miles) NW of Castledawson, County Derry, on A6. Admission charge. Open 10am-4pm daily, Easter-Sept. Tel. (01648) 33691.*

***Blennerville Windmill:** 3 km (2 miles) SW of Tralee. Admission charge. Open 10am-6pm Mon-Sat, 2pm-6pm Sun, Apr-Oct. Tel. (066) 21064.*

***Tachumshane Windmill:** 18 km (11 miles) SE of Wexford, near Lady's Island Lake. Admission free. Open daily, all year. Key from next door shop.*

OUGHAL, COUNTY CORK

he story of this medieval sailing port, from Viking imes and continuing through the building of the nglo-Norman town walls, is told well in the new **eritage Centre** on the quays. Sir Walter Raleigh, who vas the Mayor of Youghal in 1588/89, planted the first otatoes in Ireland here, and also introduced tobacco moking. Youghal had a strong tradition of sailing chooners which lasted until the mid-1930s and the entre has a fine model of a square-rigged ship. The evelopment of the town as a seaside resort in the 8th c. is also highlighted.

Many interesting places can be visited in the town. irectly opposite the centre, which also doubles as the ourist information office, is the Moby Dick pub, with hotographs taken when *Moby Dick* was filmed in oughal in 1954. The town walls on the heights behind he Main Street, are Derry's excepted, the finest in reland. Myrtle Grove, once Raleigh's house, can also e visited. Many medieval buildings, including the 777 Clock Tower, are dotted along the 1.6 km (1 mile) ong Main Street. Finally, it's worth seeing the old hotographs of the schooners on display in the Devonshire Arms Hotel.

***Heritage Centre:** Admission charge. Open 9.30am-1pm, 2pm-6pm Mon-Sat, June-Sept, 9.30am-1pm, 2pm-5.30pm Mon-Fri, Oct-May. Tel. (024) 92390.*

***Myrtle Grove House:** By arr with TIO, tel. (024) 92390.*

INDEX